Tullahoma

The 1863 Campaign for the Control of Middle Tennessee

By

Michael R. Bradley

BURD STREET PRESS

Special thanks to Mrs. Joyce Bateman, Interlibrary Loan Desk of the Crouch Library, at Motlow College in Lynchburg, Tennessee.

This Burd Street Press publication
was printed by
Beidel Printing House, Inc.
63 West Burd Street
Shippensburg, PA 17257-0152 USA

In respect for the scholarship contained herein, the acid-free paper used in this book meets the guidelines for permanence and durability of the Committee on Production Guidelines for Book Longevity of the Council on Library Resources.

For a complete list of available publications
please write
Burd Street Press
Division of White Mane Publishing Company, Inc.
P.O. Box 152
Shippensburg, PA 17257-0152 USA

Library of Congress Cataloging-in-Publication Data

Bradley, Michael R. (Michael Raymond), 1940-
    Tullahoma : the 1863 campaign for the control of middle Tennessee / by Michael R. Bradley.
        p. cm.
    Includes bibliographical references and index.
    ISBN 1-57249-167-1 (alk. paper)
    1. Tennessee--History--Civil War, 1861-1865--Campaigns. 2. Tullahoma Region (Tenn.)--History, Military--19th century. 3. United States--History--Civil War, 1861-1865--Campaigns. I. Title.

E475.16 .B73 2000
973.7'3'0976864--dc21
                                                                99-054334

To
Nancy Todd Bradley Warren
and Michael Lee Bradley
who grew up inside the outpost
line of Fort Rains in Tullahoma

Contents

Illustrations

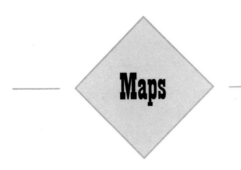

Maps

Chapter One
The Situation

Eighteen sixty-two had been a roller coaster year for Americans whether they called themselves citizens of the Union or of the Confederacy. The year had started with spectacular advances by the Union forces as General Ulysses S. Grant captured Forts Henry and Donelson, followed quickly by the fall of Nashville. This first Confederate state capital to fall was also a significant manufacturing center and was the gateway to middle Tennessee, an area rich in food, fodder, and Confederate recruits. These Union successes stood up even under the sledgehammer counterattack the Confederates mounted at Shiloh. By the time of that battle, however, New Orleans had fallen to the Union navy and, in the east, General George B. McClellan was using that same Union navy to move his army from the suburbs of Washington, D.C., to the peninsula of Virginia, where soon he would be within sight of the church steeples of Richmond.

Then the pendulum began to swing. Confederate delaying tactics and the innate caution of Union General Henry Halleck, who was called "Old Brains" but who lacked the sense to push a defeated foe, erased the immediate value of what Grant had done. Suddenly, General Stonewall Jackson was everywhere at once in the Shenandoah, and several Union generals found themselves the victims of his strategic brilliance. Shortly thereafter, the newly appointed commander of the Confederate forces in Virginia, General Robert E. Lee, had McClellan running for seven days through the James River bottoms, and General Braxton Bragg, of much maligned memory, loaded his men on railroad cars and had them in Chattanooga, bound for Kentucky, before the Union forces were fully aware of his plans. Lee had whipped Major General John Pope at Second Manassas and was heading into Maryland in step with Bragg's move. Bloody and inconclusive fighting at Sharpsburg and Perryville stopped both Confederate advances and the war came back to scenes already familiar.

The year ended with more blood in the mud as Lee thrashed General Ambrose E. Burnside at Fredericksburg, Va., and Bragg met General William S. Rosecrans at Murfreesboro, Tenn., on the banks of Stones River.

But even as the year ended the nature of the war changed. Pressured by the left wing of his own party and fearful of foreign recognition brought about by Confederate military successes, President Lincoln had given those in rebellion ninety days to rejoin the Union. If they did not do so, they would be punished by having their slaves set free.

Lincoln had the right idea, at least in part. Slavery had been a major cause of the war, indeed, without slavery all the other contributing causes could most likely have been compromised. But the strident Abolitionist voices which yammered that slavery should end immediately were quickly countered by the insistent Fire-Eaters who demanded legal guarantees which would perpetuate slavery. Between them, these two extremes destroyed all chance of the evolutionary process which had ended slavery in New York and Pennsylvania, leaving only John Brown's solution for the South—a bloodbath.

But if Lincoln was right about slavery as a major cause of the war he was wrong about the peculiar institution being a motivating force inspiring Southerners to fight. Too few Southerners owned slaves, ten percent or a little less in 1860, and most Confederate soldiers were not at all interested in risking their lives for a rich man's economic advantage. The threat of losing their slaves meant nothing to these men, they had none. Those who did hold slaves did not trust Lincoln not to take away their slaves even if they did rejoin the Union. They knew that during the 1860 presidential campaign he favored limiting the area open to slavery, but now he was calling for selective emancipation. To them, he was just another politician who changed his opinion as frequently as he changed his shirt.

Nor were Confederates the only ones to distrust Lincoln. Many Union generals and a lot of their soldiers were Democrats and for a large number of these men the war was about preserving the Union. They, no doubt, had been relieved to hear Lincoln say in 1861 "My enemies say this war is about slavery. I tell my friends it is about preserving the Union."[1] Now many of these men felt bitter, even betrayed. They were from the Midwest and although the old Northwest—Ohio, Indiana, Illinois, Wisconsin, and Michigan—had always been free states thanks to the Northwest Ordinance of 1787, these men were hardly champions of racial equality. None of their states recognized free Negroes as citizens or granted them equal rights in 1863. It is a hard fact that in nineteenth-century America the belief in White supremacy was nigh universal. These Northern men did not see themselves as a mighty army of the Lord bringing redemption to the captives, they had not joined the army to fight for freedom for Negroes. Research in the letters and diaries of these Union soldiers reveals a wide vein of disgust with the proclamation. A soldier from Illinois wrote home saying: "I am the Boy that can fight for my country, but not for negroes." A member of the 7th Kentucky Infantry, U.S., said he had "volunteered to fight to restore the old constitution & not to free negroes." From the Army of the Tennessee an Indiana private wrote his father to say he and his friends "will not fight to free the niger." Such attitudes were not confined to the midwestern soldiers but were found among New Englanders as well as midwestern civilians. On January 25, 1863, following receipt of casualty lists from Murfreesboro, John Kinsel of Hancock County, Ohio, wrote to his brother and sister-in-law. "I am getting tired of this war. I think some of the Abolitionists are getting their eyes open. I think it is an awful thing the way our young men are getting killed for the sake of a few headstrong men. I don't see as we have gained anything by all the fighting yet. But I do know we have lost a great many good men already, and probably will lose a good many more yet."[2]

Lincoln's Emancipation Proclamation of January 1, 1863, declared all slaves behind Confederate lines to be free, but those in the territory he actually controlled Lincoln left enslaved. U.S. commanders understood the true nature of the proclamation and ordered only slaves of those loyal to the Confederacy to be impressed to do labor for the Union army. The slaves of "loyal" men were left undisturbed and under the authority of their owners. The commander of the Department of the Ohio issued General Order #53 on April 28, 1863, from his Cincinnati headquarters, declaring it illegal to help any slave of a loyal man to run away or to prevent any loyal man from reclaiming his slaves. However, it was also illegal for any pro-Confederate person to keep or to sell slaves.[3] In the Tennessee theatre, Rosecrans and his subordinates perceived the Emancipation Proclamation not to be a means of freeing slaves so much as a device by which their labor could be denied to the Confederate armed forces and to their supporters. Slaves were not seen so much as human beings to be supported and cherished as brothers but as an economic commodity, one of the sinews of war, to be denied an enemy. This attitude of "pragmatic emancipation" came to permeate the entire Army of the Cumberland. In writing to his wife, James Connolly said, "Now what do you think of your husband degenerating from a conservative young Democrat to a horse stealer and a 'nigger thief', and practicing his nefarious occupation almost within gun shot of the sacred 'Hermitage' and tomb of Andrew Jackson? Yes, while in the field I am an Abolitionist; my government has decided to wipe out slavery, and I am for the government and its policy whether right or wrong, so long as its flag is confronted by the hostile guns of slavery."[4]

Of course, this policy had mixed results for the ex-slaves. In many cases the impressed slaves of Confederate owners were not paid wages by the Federal forces but were given food rations for themselves only. This meant their families were dependent for support on pro-Confederate owners who had been deprived of their major male work force. A case in point is the petition submitted to General Thomas Rousseau in March 1864. "The bearer of this was forced by order of Genl Wood (from his master-W.C. Smartt of Warren Co. Tenn) for the purpose of driving some stock from McMinnville to this place and has not been home since. He wishes to get a pass to return to his family living near McMinnville. If you can consistently grant him a pass it would not only gratify the boy but would confer a favor upon his Master who has some 25 negroes principally women and Children. . . His wife has come down a few days since to see him & wishes her pass approved."[5] In time, Union authorities would be forced to issue food to the suffering families of these impressed slaves, though they would deny food to Confederate women and children.

Some of the slaves understood the emotion of freedom better than they did the reality of their situation. Freedom and liberty did not necessarily mean the same thing under the Union plan as the following illustrates: "General Rousseau, My negro man Jim Hodge came to my house and cut up at a desperate [sic] rate, disputed my word five or six times, drew a little wagon tongue to strike me with & said he asked me no odds and that he would have my hill cleaned up in less than three days. I would like to have him arrested and carried to Nashville and put in the service of the government or deal with him as you see proper. Signed, Alexander Hodge, Bedford County, Tenn."[6] An unnamed Negro man in the Mulberry community of Lincoln County, Tennessee, learned that emancipation certainly did not mean revenge on slaveowners. Colonel Silas Colgrave, commander of the Union troops at Tullahoma, Tennessee, reported to the XII Army Corps command that he had sent a detachment to Mulberry to arrest guerrillas in connection with an attack on a party from the 9th Ohio Artillery. No guerrillas were caught, but a Negro man was brought back under arrest. A certain Mrs. Jenny Tully had been suspected of helping the guerrillas and, if this were proven, her barn and outbuildings were to have been burned. Since no proof was produced to this effect the

Union soldiers refused to fire her property. However, the unnamed Negro man set fire to the barn of Mrs. Tulley because one of the Tulley relatives had sent his wife south. The Union forces promptly arrested the man and brought him to the provost guardhouse in Tullahoma since he was not authorized to burn the property and had merely taken personal revenge for a personal wrong.[7]

The views of General Rosecrans on the topic of emancipation did not become clearly known for several weeks and, when they did, it was in the curious context of his being sounded out as a possible candidate for the presidency. The probe of his willingness to be president had begun in April 1863 when the general sent an open letter to several states throughout the Midwest. In the face of increasing talk that Lincoln was merely a "widow maker" and with secret societies working for peace with an independent Confederacy, he stated, "This war is for the maintainence of the Constitution and the laws. I am amazed that anyone can think of peace on any terms. He who entertains the sentiment is fit only to be a slave; he who utters it is a traitor to his country."

In Ohio, where Clement Vallandigham was about to become governor, the legislature refused to allow the letter to be printed. In Washington, Secretary of War Stanton was infuriated, thinking Rosecrans planned to become the hero of the Radicals and be made president either by election or by coup. Some talk of a coup was actually in the offing. Horace Greely, of the New York *Tribune*, had lost confidence in Lincoln even though he had backed his nomination and election. Lincoln had twice mentioned resigning and now Greely looked on Rosecrans as the only universally successful Union general. The newspaperman wanted Lincoln to step down and Vice President Hannibal Hamlin to name the general commander of all Union armies. From this post the step to the presidency would be easy if he would openly oppose slavery. His open letter spoke of supporting the Constitution, but it did not address the issue of slavery.

To tease an answer out of Rosecrans, Greely sent his old friend James A. Gilmore, a merchant and writer. In a private conversation Rosecrans told Gilmore "The Negro should be given a Bible, a spelling book, freedom, and a chance for something more than six feet of earth. Then he should be left alone." That was the sort of answer Greely wanted but it was still a private answer. On April 27 Rosecrans went public in a letter to the editor of the *Catholic Telegraph* of Cincinnati. The editor was congratulated "on the splendid stand you take against slavery. Slavery is dead." This letter was promptly reprinted in the *Tribune*.

General Rosecrans was opposed to slavery, favored an end to the institution, but did not go so far as the Radicals who advocated racial equality. This looked to be a good political position which would have wide appeal among voters of many views, but when Gilmore asked the key question, Rosecrans said, "No." He was a soldier and such he would remain.[8]

Confederate supporters understood the intent of the proclamation also and, in some cases, tried to move slaves to the South. Dr. J. A. Blackmore was serving with the Confederate army near Shelbyville, Tenn., in December 1862. He wrote to his wife at Gallatin, behind Union lines: "I would like to have Bockus and Matt here as they are doing nothing there. I have learned they would not come when I sent for them fearing I would sell them, assure them I have no intention if they behave themselves, whether they come or not. Buy and send the young black man you mentioned as the Yankees will take him.[9]

Some retaliated on their Unionist neighbors who owned slaves by seizing their slaves. Just after the end of the war, F. A. Silvertooth of Coffee County, Tennessee, was charged by the military authorities of having gone to the home of "J.J. Mankins and confiscated his negras and took them to his house while Mankins was in the Union Army."[10] Others simply left their slaves to take care of themselves, and of their owner's property, while the owner went south as a refugee. In May 1865, three slaves of Gabriel Maupin of Bedford County, Tennessee, petitioned General George Thomas to be allowed to stay where their old master had left them. They said, "After the said Gabriel Maupin ran South and abandoned his plantation they had no place to stay at except on said plantation and they stayed there and worked and made a support for themselves . . . Petitioners would further state that although their old Master the said Gabriel Maupin was a very great Rebel and aided and assisted and sympathised with the so called Confederacy yet when he was about to leave he requested and desired his Slaves petitioners to stay on the plantation and work it and try and support themselves."[11]

For the most part, the Emancipation Proclamation caused little stir in Bragg's army or in the area where it operated, at least on the surface. In the mind of Major General Patrick Cleburne an idea was germinating, a plan was being developed. Before the Tullahoma campaign opened Cleburne discussed with several of his brigadiers a plan for freeing slaves and enrolling them in the Confederate forces. During the winter of 1863-64 this plan became widely discussed and was extremely controversial. At any rate, using Black men as military assets in the front lines was an idea not confined to Union minds.

The situation for 1863 was a demanding one. Union armies must win enough victories to assure those in the North who were not interested in emancipation that the war was being won and that the Union would be preserved. At the same time, victories were necessary to convince foreign powers that emancipation was an achievable goal and not merely political posturing on the part of a wounded president and administration who were losing a war or, at least, who were caught in a military stalemate. The pressure was on Union commanders during 1863.

While the men of the opposing armies worked out what they would consider an appropriate reaction to the Emancipation Proclamation, two commanders had more immediate and pragmatic considerations. Generals William Rosecrans and Braxton Bragg each had a feud on their hands: Rosecrans with the War Department and Bragg with his generals.

Obviously, the Union War Department understood why the Lincoln administration needed victories so badly and one response was to pressure field commanders to take action. In Virginia, this resulted in the aptly named "Mud March" when General Burnside tried to move the Army of the Potomac up the Rappahannock to flank the Confederate position he had tried so disastrously to overrun in December. Grant made a move toward Vicksburg only to be thwarted by a cavalry raid on his supply base at Holly Springs, Mississippi. This raid, led by Major General Earl Van Dorn, left Grant a long ways from home base at Memphis with not enough to eat or to shoot. It also left General William T. Sherman all alone to bloody his nose by butting his head against the Confederate earthworks at Chickasaw Bayou. Considering those debacles Rosecrans must have felt rather pleased at what he had achieved in the battle along the banks of Stones River and have felt it appropriate to sit quietly at Murfreesboro which allowed his troops to move into winter quarters. Actually, a number of these troops were put to work building fortifications, the largest of which is today known as Fort Rosecrans.

This relative inaction on the part of a major field force did not set well with the Union commander, Henry Halleck. Although in April and May 1862 he had moved against Corinth with all the speed and agility of a turtle wading through molasses, Halleck expected Rosecrans to defeat a leading Confederate ally, mud, so as to advance through middle Tennessee in the dead of winter. Tennessee winters are not noted for being especially cold but they are notorious for being wet. Rosecrans took a much more realistic view of the situation and set himself to wait for the roads to dry out with the coming of spring.

Lieutenant General Braxton Bragg

This is an early war likeness.

Major General William S. Rosecrans

Chickamauga-Chattanooga National Battlefield Park

If a major army could not move, small units could and soon the country was swarming with units of Confederate cavalry, regular and irregular. These units made life miserable for Rosecrans—they captured mail coaches, wrecked trains, cut off couriers and foraging parties, and virtually closed the railroads as far north as central Kentucky. In the western theatre small unit cavalry forays were a Confederate forte, and such men as Wheeler, Forrest, Morgan, and Van Dorn may as well have been issued a patent on that type of action. The success of these units was very much like that of the Liliputians against Gulliver—no one raid or ambush did much damage but the cumulative effect was to immobilize Rosecrans so that he was truly fast stuck in the mud.

Halleck decided to remedy this situation by long distance. If the Confederate raiders made life miserable for Rosecrans, Halleck made it unbearable! By letter, by dispatch, by telegram, and by courier Halleck began to bombard the general with unsolicited and impractical advice mixed with moralizing and not a little pomposity. Whether the issue was a matter of strategy, supplies, arms, or authority Halleck knew just what Rosecrans should do and he told him so, in great detail and with copious citations from army regulations. Never a man to run away from a good argument, the general replied in kind, adding liberal doses of common sense and moral philosophy to what he wanted to say. Soon, the two men were engaged in a dispute which would have done great credit to spoiled three year olds in a back-yard sandbox.

The Union army was plagued with desertions. The weather was bad, the army at a standstill, and home was not too far away for many of his men. When such men could be caught, Rosecrans wanted authority to court-martial them and, if found guilty, to shoot them on the spot. Halleck turned down the idea saying the law required that the president review all death sentences. The general felt the president was so faraway as to make review too slow. If a lesson was to be taught, trial and execution needed to be swift. Besides, the president was noted for his leniency. Halleck saw only the law. He could not, or would not, sympathize with Rosecrans.[12]

Because of the activity of the Confederate cavalry units and their negative impact on his supply lines, Rosecrans felt compelled to build up his mounted arm, and the winter was the time to do this. He expressed his needs clearly. "Cavalry horses are indispensible to our success here. We have always been without the control of the country, except for a short distance beyond our infantry lines, and all the horses and forage the country could furnish have thus fallen into the hands of the enemy. They subsist upon the country by having five to one of our mounted force. Out of our nominal cavalry force we have not more than forty percent available for want of horses."[13] Rosecrans was soon asking for horses from Nashville, Louisville, and Washington. His reply was to make his requests through proper channels and to stop asking other commanders for help. Quartermaster General Montgomery C. Meigs apparently felt Rosecrans had impugned his ability to provide supplies, and joined the fray by sending him a lengthy lecture, a missive which is a monument of pedantry, telling Rosecrans to cease his continuous and "unreasonable" demands for horses. Meigs concluded that Rosecrans had received 19,164 horses and 23,859 mules. These should be enough to move the army if he would just learn to take care of them properly, Meigs concluded.[14] Now the War Department was haranguing the commander of one of its major field armies about animal husbandry.

Rosecrans lost little time in returning fire, using double loads of sarcasm. Politely he stated that Meigs needed to learn how to count, for his letter showed he had "fallen into quite a number of errors on the subject." Rosecrans claimed to have on hand 8,475 horses for cavalry and mounted infantry combined. Of these, 2,119 were not fit for duty; of the remainder more than three thousand were used by orderlies, escorts, and the garrison of Nashville. This left him only 3,003 properly mounted troopers.[15] No wonder the Confederates owned the countryside.

Halleck was not about to let Rosecrans have the last shot in this verbal war. Did he think the government could pick money off a tree? Did the general in Murfreesboro know what a horse cost, or how much the government had already spent on his army? Did he understand how much it cost to keep his force in the field even for one day? At this hectoring, Rosecrans exploded. If Halleck thought horses were expensive, why did he send only half enough to do the job, thereby guaranteeing the effort would have to be made at least twice? If horse flesh was valuable, what about human flesh? Rosecrans was risking the lives and well-being of his men because he did not have enough animals to scout and to protect his lines from raids. If Halleck was concerned about the cost of the war he should give Rosecrans what he needed to end the business for that would save money in the long run. Halleck then replied with a complaint about the cost of Rosecrans' telegraph bills, saying he spent as much money on the telegraph as all the rest of the generals in all the other armies combined.[16]

As spring came to middle Tennessee and as the armies in Virginia and Mississippi began their campaigns, the volume of messages to Rosecrans increased and the pressure to move mounted. Against it all, Rosecrans stood firm. When he had cavalry and mounted infantry, properly armed and mounted, when he had supplies and a secure base, then he would move. Then, and not before.

Bragg did not have to worry about the Confederate War Department, he had support there. Bragg's feud was with his corps and division commanders. Dissatisfaction with his leadership was, in part, based on his personality, for he was not a man who engendered affection. Of course, in an age when travel was largely by horseback, a man who suffered from ulcerated hemorrhoids was entitled to have a bad disposition, and such was rumored to have been the case with Bragg. His mindset was a curious combination of indecision and rigidity, and this indecision often hampered him in making both strategic and tactical decisions. But reaching a decision he refused to change his mind to meet changing circumstances. Bragg tended to be harsh with his friends and impossible with his opponents. Although destruction of the enemy on the battlefield is an end to be desired, in human relations leaving a graceful line of retreat often smooths matters. Such a tactic was not for Bragg. When confronted with criticism or opposition he tried to crush and humiliate those against him. He never seemed to have understood the amount of venom which was generated by injured pride.[17]

Widespread discontent had begun to show itself during and after the Kentucky campaign of 1862. During that late summer and autumn Bragg seemed to have several chances to discommode the Federal forces, but at Munfordville he stepped back and left the road open for Major General Don Carlos Buell to escape to Louisville after capturing a small garrison, and at Perryville a total misreading of the Union strategy had left him with a tactical victory which led to another strategic retreat. As his hungry and footsore men clambered down from Cumberland Gap towards Knoxville, the soon-to-be-familiar motto began to be heard, "Bully for Bragg. He's hell on retreat." As the Army of Tennessee fell back through the rain after the battle at Murfreesboro the feeling grew stronger among the men that their valor and blood had bought a battlefield victory which Bragg's lack of ability had thrown away. Defeat was snatched from the jaws of victory! Most of the general officers agreed with this point of view as did at least one influential area newspaper.

On January 10, 1863, Bragg assembled his staff and read to them an editorial from the Chattanooga *Rebel* which was critical of his management of the battle of Murfreesboro. After reading the editorial to them Bragg asked if he should resign. It must have struck like a twelve-pounder shell when his staff answered, "Yes." However, being a glutton for punishment, Bragg drafted a letter to his corps and division commanders asking two things: did they agree with the decision to retreat from Murfreesboro, and did Bragg have the confidence of the army? If he did not have the confidence of the army, he would resign. Soon the answers began to come in. Lieutenant General William Hardee replied that he and his two major generals, Patrick Cleburne and John Breckenridge, agreed that Bragg should resign, not only that, all the brigadiers in both divisions agreed with their superior officers. Lieutenant General Leonidas Polk was away from the army on leave but there was no doubt in Bragg's mind what Polk thought. Likewise, the negative opinions of Polk's Division commanders, Benjamin F. Cheatham and John McCown, were also known. When Polk returned to the army at the end of January, Bragg told him not to bother replying. General Joseph E. Johnston was at headquarters at the time in his capacity as department commander. In a letter to Jefferson Davis, Johnston said that Polk and Hardee both lacked confidence in Bragg as did many subordinate generals. Johnston thought the troops willing to fight were confident in their own ability; the key was the question of Davis' confidence in Bragg.[18]

Within a few days Davis wrote back to Johnston, expressing confidence in Bragg but reminding Johnston that his position as department commander gave him the authority to take direct command of the army if he thought necessary. Bragg took this expression of presidential confidence as reason for him to go on the offensive. Instead of retreating, he would attack; instead of resigning he would drive his opposition out of the army.[19] In this attack he appears to have adopted a "take no prisoners, bayonet the wounded" attitude toward his opponents, but he did not look at the odds against him. Quite soon Bragg was leveling criticism at Major General John Breckenridge for the attack he had made at McFadden's Ford on January 2 at the Murfreesboro battle, and he was also tasking Cheatham for taking too many casualties, probably because Cheatham was drunk. It is true Breckenridge had gone far beyond his orders on January 2 and had led his men in a "charge of the Light Brigade" into the muzzles of some four dozen cannon. It is also true that Cheatham liked whiskey although one would never have known he was a heavy drinker unless one had happened to see him sober. True charges or not, both these men had powerful political friends and Bragg was inviting trouble by attacking them.[20]

Naturally, Bragg thought he was adopting the proper course. In late February he wrote to a close friend, Colonel B. S. Ewell, to say dissatisfaction was disappearing in the army. The whole affair was the fault of "disappointed generals, who supposed they could cover their tracks and rise on my downfall." After this event, he would not give so much leeway to men who were older than he but who were his junior in rank. To make sure these corps commanders did not get much leeway Bragg wrote his report of the Kentucky campaign, a report filed May 20, 1863, in a fashion which was critical of both men. Polk was charged with disobedience of orders at both Bardstown and Perryville, charges Polk took seriously enough to begin gathering material to defend himself at a court-martial, and he also allowed an unauthorized copy of his Perryville report, which refuted Bragg, to be printed in the Knoxville *Register.*[21]

Bragg also went after General John McCown. At Murfreesboro, McCown had failed to execute his orders correctly in the opening attack and had allowed the next unit in line to his right to be flanked, and the attack held up. Since taking up position along the Duck River he had also disregarded Bragg's orders against detaching officers for duty at distant posts. These things alone might not have led to a court-martial except for the fact that McCown was openly opposed to Bragg. These matters had been pending against McCown for some time and he was, naturally, anxious to defend himself, so he called up his political heavy artillery. Representatives H. S. Foote and G. A. Henry called on President Davis and asked him to speed up the process of McCown's trial. The general was much beloved by his men, they said, and he was wanted back at his division. Of course, McCown had served in the state militia for many years and had become close allies with Foote and Henry. Bragg had again kicked open a political nest of yellow jackets, so McCown got his trial if not the result he wanted.[22]

On March 16, 1863, a court-martial convened at Shelbyville with Major General Cleburne as its senior officer. This put Cleburne in a rather awkward position because it was his division which had been left exposed when McCown failed to carry out his orders at Murfreesboro. Cleburne was not only one of McCown's judges, he would vote on his fate as if he were a juryman and would also have knowledge which would make him a good witness for the prosecution. The charges and specifications against McCown were so obviously true that the court had no choice but to find him guilty and to suspend him from command for six months. In the end, McCown never returned to the Army of Tennessee.[23] Bragg had destroyed one of his targets.

Polk was not deterred. Shortly after McCown left the army Polk wrote President Davis that Bragg had great talent in organizing and training troops; therefore, he should be made inspector general of the Confederate armies so as to be able to exercise those talents. However, Polk insisted that General Joseph Johnston should be named to command in the field. Colonel Preston Johnston, son of the dead Sidney Johnston, agreed with that opinion.[24] At the time Bragg apparently was satisfied with the pound of flesh he had sliced from McCown and did not pursue the vendetta, for once allowing his penchant for incomplete victories to serve his army well. Clearly, the issue was not resolved. The bickering among the high command would continue with Breckenridge being sent to Mississippi and other officers spending time writing charges and countercharges against each other when they should have been planning how to defeat Rosecrans. Eventually, in December 1863, Bragg would be replaced but the Army of Tennessee would go into the Tullahoma campaign with a high command splintered into fragments.[25] If the generals had fought Rosecrans and the Army of the Cumberland with the same diligence as they fought each other, and had they concentrated on spilling Yankee blood instead of printer's ink, the campaign might have had a different ending.

Both generals had more to do than fight those who stood behind them, however. They had to get ready to fight each other, and the most pressing problem both men faced was to supply men and animals with food. If stomachs could not be filled, men and mules could not march very far or very long.

Rosecrans had the pressing necessity of feeding 100,000 men and 50,000 horses and mules in an area stripped almost bare by two years of war. Stretching out behind Rosecrans as a supply line were more than 200 miles of rail line highly vulnerable to Confederate attack, and 250 miles of roads which became nearly impassable in winter. As an example of the vulnerability of the railroad, from July 1, 1862, to July 1, 1863, trains ran on the Louisville and Nashville Railroad, the primary supply line, only seven months and twelve days. Every bridge on the line was destroyed and rebuilt at least once and some of them three or four times.[26] The rail line passed through twin tunnels at Gallatin, Tennessee, and at one time these tunnels were plugged with debris for a distance of 800 feet. If they could be destroyed the road could be closed for as much as six weeks, as Confederate raider John Morgan had proved in 1862. A major trestle, and therefore a major Confederate target, was at Muldraughs Hill in Kentucky. In between these two major targets were numerous rivers and creeks, all with bridges or culverts which could be cut and many steep grades where slow-moving trains could be ambushed. Even the destruction of a few water tanks where the boilers for steam engines were refilled could disable the line for a time.

If the railroad was vulnerable it was at least speedy, or seemed so by the standards of that day. A train could travel 20 or 30 miles per hour and could stay on the go around the clock with only occasional stops for fuel and water; the train crews ate while the engines were cared for. Wagons, traveling by road, had speeds more in the three- to five-mile-per-hour range, if that, and the day's travel was limited by the muscle endurance of the draft animals. Both speed and endurance declined for wagon travel in winter weather because of road conditions.

Middle Tennessee had few good roads. A decent network of all-weather pikes radiated from Nashville, but the hard road surface usually stopped only a few miles out of town. After that, the road was a combination of red clay—dust or mud, depending on the season—and limestone rock, generally of an inconvenient size. A few miles from Nashville the roads climbed a ragged but steep escarpment called the Highland Rim. This "Highland Rim" stretches completely around Nashville which is located in the Cumberland Basin. Therefore, one clambers down into or up out of Nashville. On this road net wintertime speeds of one mile per hour were common and prolonged rain or brief snows could close off road travel completely.

Supplementing this road net was the Cumberland River. Flowing west by northwest out of Nashville, the Cumberland passes Clarksville and Dover—site of Fort Donelson—before reaching the Ohio near Paducah, Kentucky. Following the capture of Fort Donelson in February 1862, the Cumberland had become a Union highway funneling men and supplies into middle Tennessee behind the iron walls of riverine gunboats. But this highway, too, was vulnerable. The Cumberland was not a big river; in dry weather it might be too shallow for navigation, and in wet weather the current could hold back upstream traffic, at all times boats could be reached by gunfire from either bank. Since many Union gunboats had been withdrawn for service on the Mississippi and elsewhere, transports made tempting targets for guerrillas or the horse artillery of Confederate cavalry.

Rosecrans had good reason to keep glancing over his shoulder as he confronted Bragg. A vulnerable supply line made any advance quite risky and Bragg set out to increase that risk.

Less than three weeks after his victory at Murfreesboro, Rosecrans began to feel the pinch in his supplies. Colonel A. S. Hall had taken a train of wagons out the Liberty Pike from Murfreesboro on a foraging expedition. A sudden attack by Confederate guerrillas cost him his train, and Rosecrans held the colonel responsible for the loss and suffering of his command. Soon, Colonel Hall would have plenty of company. Within the same week Rosecrans reported he was having to use as much as a brigade of infantry to escort wagon trains between Murfreesboro and Nashville. At the same time the post commander at LaVergne was reporting Wheeler's entire command was between the Nolensville and Murfreesboro Pikes and nearer to Nashville than to LaVergne.[27] This means Wheeler was 30 miles behind the Union army and in position to cut rail lines, turn-pikes, and interdict river traffic. Captain B. W. Canfield, 105th Ohio Infantry, was dismissed from the service for losing his train of 34 wagons, 184 animals, and 164 men to "a scarcely superior force of the enemy." Canfield was lucky to escape with a dishonorable dis-charge for Rosecrans stated in the dismissal order that he regretted he could not have him shot.[28] Lines of supply were clearly a touchy subject with the commanding general. Somewhat luckier were Cap-tain Stein, 6th Kentucky Infantry, and Lieutenant Cameron, 110th Ohio Infantry. They received a Valentine's Day public reprimand for allowing a portion of a forage train to be captured. They were saved from worse disgrace because they were not in overall command of the expedition.[29]

Rosecrans found some relief when an attack on Fort Donelson by Wheeler, with Forrest in a subordinate role, failed in late Febru-ary, but he was still quite uneasy about his supply line. It seemed to him the river would be easier to defend and would demand less in resources and manpower to keep open than would the railroad. While demanding more cavalry, Rosecrans began to call loudly for more gunboats to protect convoys of steamboats bringing supplies to Nashville. If more gunboats could not be furnished, Rosecrans said on March 6, he would soon run out of supplies.[30]

Still the problems continued. In early March General George Crook wrote from Carthage, Tennessee, that 18 wagons and two companies of the 18th Ohio Infantry had been captured by approxi-mately 140 guerrillas. In the rough terrain of the country around Carthage, Crook said he could not operate without gunboats on the river and cavalry for the hills. A few days later, and 100 miles in the opposite direction, a train was derailed near Bowling Green, Ken-tucky, by 40 or 50 Confederate cavalry.[31] In April, Confederate forces wrecked a train on the Kentucky state line at Franklin, again block-ing the line. Soon afterwards Brigadier General Erasmus A. Paine, commanding U.S. forces at Gallatin, Tennessee, reported track torn up and Confederates prowling around the twin tunnels. The next week a steamboat was fired into by pro-Confederate citizens and the boat sank after hitting a log.[32] In the days just preceding the opening of the Tullahoma campaign 18 men were lost when the U.S. mail was attacked at Hartsville, Tennessee, and 175 mules were captured not far from Nashville on the Gallatin Pike.[33]

None of this made Rosecrans' task impossible but it made the job much more difficult causing the commanding general endless worry, much of which he passed up and down the chain of com-mand in bad-tempered correspondence. Certainly, the clogged condi-tion of his line of supply made the accumulation of a reserve of food for a forward movement a constant burden for Rosecrans.

Having food at all, much less a surplus, was a constant burden for the Confederate army as well. In the years after the war, one old Confederate veteran was heard to remark, "They wuz two sides in that war; they wuz th' Feds—that wuz them, and they wuz th' unfeds— that wuz us." The condition of the Army of Tennessee during the opening months of 1863 gave credence to that memory.

The position Bragg occupied made his supply situation worse. In order to block the Nashville and Chattanooga Railroad, Bragg held a roughly north-south line. This placed within his lines part of the Highland Rim area and the Cumberland Plateau, neither of them the most productive agricultural areas. The more fertile Tennessee River Valley in east Tennessee was not available to feed Bragg's army because foodstuffs from there, as well as from Georgia, were all designated for Lee's Army of Northern Virginia. This meant the Army of Tennessee benefitted very little, so far as food was concerned, from its rail link to Chattanooga, Knoxville, and Atlanta. The army was expected to feed itself from the Cumberland Basin, much of which was Union occupied or was no-man's-land, and the rest of which was protected only by a screen of cavalry which extended from Shelbyville, on Bragg's left flank, all the way to Columbia, about 50 miles. Even though Bragg had 12,000 to 14,000 cavalry, this protective screen would be thin since he had also to protect his right flank and keep some force in hand for forays against Union supply lines. This also meant food supplies had to be collected and brought in by wagon train because no functioning railroad served the area. There was a railroad from Nashville to Decatur, Alabama, and this town, in turn, had rail links to Chattanooga. A haul of approximately 200 miles by rail, along the Confederate-controlled portions of these lines, would still have delivered supplies to the Army of Tennessee faster than could be done by wagon. Unfortunately, several missing bridges made most of the Nashville to Decatur road useless.

As early as the end of January 1863, General Joseph E. Johnston was wiring Richmond that supplies of food, especially meat, were so reduced in middle Tennessee it was necessary to draw rations from Atlanta. A short and sharp reply was soon returned by Commissary General Lucius Northrop. The rations in Atlanta were for the use of the Army of Northern Virginia only; moreover, the Army of Tennessee must have been wasting food by issuing it in excess of regulation amounts. Everybody in Richmond knew the state of Tennessee produced plenty of food.[34] Johnston, Bragg, and the Army of Tennessee knew this was not true, so they all began to look for makeshift solutions.

Johnston suggested that while the weather remained cold the army be issued beef on the hoof, a very agreeable dish, and that hogs be sent to northern Georgia to be slaughtered and salted. In warm weather the army could then receive salt pork. Instead, the commissary at Richmond insisted the Tennessee army should get fresh pork and have salt beef, which no one much liked, during the hot weather. While trying to vary the diet of the forces Johnston also gave orders for the Memphis and Charleston Railroad to be repaired between Bridgeport and Decatur, Alabama. This would help speed supplies from northern Alabama.[35]

Such makeshift solutions would help but there was one stark fact staring the western Confederates in the face. With the country behind them dedicated to producing supplies for Virginia and with the country before them occupied by Yankees they had no means for feeding themselves for much longer. Major J. J. Walker was the chief commissary officer of the Army of Tennessee and, in a long and carefully written letter to his superiors, he predicted the entire Confederacy east of the Mississippi would run out of meat by June 1, 1863, and that there would be no means to provide more except a successful invasion of Kentucky.[36] From Richmond, General Northrop replied that middle Tennessee was capable of feeding Bragg's army; the area had fed it while it was stationed around Murfreesboro. Unfortunately, the situation had changed. The most productive areas of the district were now beyond, or almost beyond, Bragg's reach. In the midst of this exchange Major Walker ordered that the salt in which meat came packed be given to the cavalry and artillery for use by the horses.[37]

As spring began to show signs of arrival Johnston tried to help Bragg widen the area from which he could feed his men by sending purchasing agents into previously untouched areas of Alabama. Major W. W. Guy established a depot at Oxford, Alabama, on the Tennessee River and Alabama Railroad as close as he could to "navigation on the Coosa River at Rome, Georgia." So far, the major said, he had collected only a few beeves but he had high hopes for the wheat crop. That left only three to four months before the army might have bread. As is always the case in hard times some were trying to take advantage of the situation. Major Guy asked for authority to confiscate foodstuffs from "speculators and wealthy planters who are hoarding it."[38]

Major A. D. Banks, assistant adjutant general, reported to Colonel B. S. Ewell, chief of staff, in Chattanooga, that he had taken a survey which led him to believe the army could be supplied from middle Tennessee until the end of April or mid-May. Lincoln, Giles, and Maury counties were thought to have a lot of surplus food with perhaps as much as 800,000 pounds of meat in Lincoln alone. Major Moses Cruse, a former Lincoln County sheriff, was being sent there to collect supplies.[39] This good news was tempered by the military situation. Maury County was at the far left end of Bragg's cavalry line and was vulnerable to attacks from Nashville and Murfreesboro by way of Franklin. Giles County was south of Maury but was open to raids from Federal forces to the southwest along the Tennessee River at Florence, Alabama. Only Lincoln County was militarily secure and before that potential supply could be tapped 400,000 rations of meat were needed immediately to carry the army until March 1. Lieutenant Colonel David Urquhart of Bragg's staff asked department headquarters at Chattanooga to make a case for this proposal in Richmond; he had just been refused by the depot in Atlanta.[40]

Meanwhile, Major J. F. Cummings was sent out to purchase food but he soon fell afoul of Johnston. The general complained that Cummings did not attend to purchasing personally but sent out agents to do the work for him. These agents were paying as much as twice the price previously offered and were using state, not Confederate, money. The state money was more popular because it could be used behind Union lines and Confederate money could not. Johnston felt this sudden doubling of prices paid producers would only encourage hoarding in expectation of even higher prices. The people who had held on to food were either disloyal or of weak loyalty else they would have sold under the old prices. Johnston wanted only Confederate money circulated and wished prices to be set locally.[41] But even as he griped about procedure, army headquarters was receiving a report from Major J. W. Goodwin who was repairing the Confederate-held portion of the Nashville and Decatur Railroad. As soon as he completed trestles over Richland Creek near Pulaski, Tennessee, and Sulphur Creek near Elkmont, Alabama, he could operate the road.[42] This would allow movement by rail from Columbia, Tennessee, to the junction with the Memphis and Charleston near Decatur and thence east to Bridgeport and then back northwest on the Nashville and Chattanooga to Bragg's supply depot at Tullahoma. With time and luck a rail net might be patched up to supply the army. Johnston wrote Adjutant General Samuel Cooper that the position of Bragg's force was "disadvantageous because for subsistence it is compelled to take ground west of the direct route from Murfreesboro to Chattanooga. It can, therefore, be turned by our right."[43]

As supplies from northern Alabama began to arrive via steamboat from Decatur and by rail from Athens the Army of Tennessee inventoried its supplies. By combining the items available at

Shelbyville, Tullahoma, and Chattanooga it was found the soldiers could count resources of 36,000 pounds of bacon, 15,000 pounds of hardtack, and 35,000 pounds of soap.[44] When an army's supply of meat is equaled by its supply of soap and when soap is twice as plentiful as hardtack the supply situation is serious. One quick response was to cut the bacon ration from twelve to eight ounces per day.[45] As Rosecrans advanced Bragg had details of men out in front of his position cutting wheat. "Finding myself amongst good people, I gave cheerful permission to my men to aid the citizens in harvesting their crops of wheat and rye and afterwards planting their corn."[46] He had to harvest the food he needed to feed his army.

The demands of war put both commanding generals in a classic dilemma. While uncertain of their ability to supply the men they had on hand they must still expend every effort to assemble yet more men. Like all generals in all wars they always wished for more. Rosecrans, of course, was more likely to get men since the Union could recruit from a much larger area with a greater manpower pool. By 1863 yet another Union advantage was beginning to kick in, enough Southern territory had been occupied to allow recruitment of Unionists and the Emancipation Proclamation stimulated recruiting among Black men.

The stereotype of Southern Unionists usually focuses on east Tennessee, but Rosecrans counted in his ranks the 1st Middle Tennessee Union Cavalry and the 1st Alabama Union Cavalry. Indeed, of Rosecran's 22 regiments of cavalry 10 had been raised in the South. He would not have the 1st Alabama for long, they would accompany Colonel Able Streight on his abortive raid into northern Alabama and Georgia and would be gobbled up by Brigadier General Nathan Bedford Forrest near Gaylesville, Alabama. During a scouting expedition east of Murfreesboro in February, General J. J. Reynolds found some pro-Union sentiment in the villages of Liberty and Alexandria. This sentiment was expressed hesitantly despite the temporary presence of Union soldiers because harsh measures had been taken by the Confederate government and local pro-Confederate residents against those who differed with them. In order to encourage more Union men to come out into the open Reynolds suggested a "harsh war" policy against all inside Union lines who would not take the Oath of Allegiance. This concept, endorsed by Generals Thomas and Rosecrans, with Halleck in agreement, was adopted. In early March, General Order #43 ordered out of the Union lines all who sympathized with the Confederacy, but, at the same time, pro-Union civilians would be protected. Captain J. Hartly, 45th Indiana Cavalry, was dishonorably discharged for permitting his men to plunder a loyal citizen. Major James Connolly noted "many wealthy, influential people in this section of Tennessee are intensely loyal, and I expect Bedford County, Tennessee, is as loyal today as many a county in Ohio.[47]

Attempts were also being made to recruit Black men, even those already employed by the Union army. There must have been a considerable number employed because in January 1863, Rosecrans announced it would be a deliberate policy to maximize the number of fighting men by employing Negroes in the quartermaster and hospital departments. Negroes who had been abandoned by owners and had gone South as refugees and those held as slaves by Confederate sympathizers were to be the first employed. Only in cases of absolute necessity were the slaves of loyal men to be employed and then the owners were to be given a receipt for the slaves taken.[48] Some might argue that such employees were not "real" soldiers, but the Union army felt differently. For every Black man placed on a wagon seat or employed loading boxcars a trained soldier could be relieved of that duty and sent to the front; and to this point, all trained soldiers were White. Of course, Black men could be trained to be soldiers but that might take as much as a year; they already knew how to drive wagons, to care for animals, and could make a contribution doing that immediately; therefore, recruiting among Black army employees was frowned on. First Lieutenant S. E. Adams, acting assistant quartermaster, complained to Colonel Mersy, commanding the Second Brigade, that eight "contrabands," who had been under his employ and who had just drawn an issue of clothing, were "enticed away by a colored Sergt called Webb to join the 32nd Alabama Colored Regiment. . . I understand the colored Sergt is here at present trying to lure others away."[49] Having found men, one still had to keep them.

Of this, Rosecrans was painfully aware. On January 30, 1863, the general reported 80,447 aggregate in his army. This report did not list his "effective" strength, but three weeks later he claimed 58,112 men "at the front." Attrition had been heavy in all units as Connolly noted about his own 123rd Illinois Infantry, "We are cut down in eight months service from 962 men to about 460, 200 of that loss being in battle and skirmish." By the end of February the difference between the number of men who could be committed to an active campaign and the number who were on the rolls of the Army of the Cumberland was more than 44,000.[50] In effect, Rosecrans had two armies, one present and the other absent. In an attempt to unite these forces he ordered all absentees without specific orders to rejoin the army at Murfreesboro, or face arrest.

Such orders had only limited effect. For one thing, there were too many civilian officials clamoring for troops to be dispatched north to help protect them against the great Confederate threat of the moment, Brigadier General John Hunt Morgan. It seemed that Morgan was momentarily expected at all points north, especially throughout Kentucky, and, indeed, it was regularly reported that he had been seen in two or three places at once. Rosecrans regularly replied to these requests that he had no men to spare, that men should be moving to him, not away from him. Nevertheless, if a Union officer and some men happened to be in these "threatened" locations the continued and impassioned requests of local civilian leaders gave them good cover not to leave their warm, dry billets to return to the cold, wet camps around Murfreesboro. Rosecrans even ordered his provost marshal to make sure the army was not paying rent to civilians in Nashville to house soldiers who should be in Murfreesboro. When apprehended, deserters were treated with severity. James Connolly, major of the 123rd Illinois, wrote to his wife that he had been assigned to defend a lieutenant of that regiment who was being court-martialed for desertion. Connolly said he would do his best even though he wanted the man punished for his actions. The lieutenant had married shortly before joining the army, had not been paid for a long time, and was quite distraught when his wife wrote to tell him their first child had been born but she was out of money. Connolly supposed the officer would be sentenced to be shot but that Lincoln would stop the execution. Colonel John Beatty, also in Murfreesboro, observed that "shaving the head and drumming out of camp is a fearful punishment. I could not help pity the poor fellow, as with carpet sack in one hand and hat in the other he marched crest-fallen through the camps to the 'Rogue's March'"[51]

If coercion was of limited use Rosecrans decided to appeal to pride. In February an order went out that an honor roll was to be established in each regiment. Commanding officers were to select three privates, five noncommissioned officers, and one commissioned officer per company who had been observed in acts of bravery and their names were to be entered on the roll. He intended to have these men mounted and provided with the very best in weapons, so they would form an elite corps to lead the advance in active campaigning. In the end this plan fell afoul of the legalisms of Halleck who told Rosecrans the field commander had no authority to separate volunteers from their state-authorized units.[52]

As the weather began to improve, detachments, men in hospital and on furlough, and general absentees began to return to the Army of the Cumberland. By the end of April, Rosecrans had 99,360 men aggregate with 38,000 still absent from the ranks.[53] He had received 14,000 men transferred from the Department of the Ohio, and seven of his subordinate generals received promotions allowing him to reorganize his army.[54] Despite his fears, Rosecrans would begin the Tullahoma campaign superior in numbers in every department, including mounted troops. The official numbers credit Rosecrans with about half the cavalry Bragg listed but the Union cavalry does not include the mounted infantry. He would begin the campaign with an aggregate of 96,000 of which about 63,000 would be present at the front; he would end the campaign with about 95,500.[55]

To whatever comment Rosecrans might have made about absentees, Bragg would surely have agreed. The Army of Tennessee was plagued by men leaving the ranks during the winter of 1863. Some of these were men who had become war weary after the retreat from Murfreesboro. As their homes came behind Union lines and hopes for a quick redemption faded, some men reexamined their priorities and found the commitment to family was stronger than their commitment to the Confederacy. Others looked at the waterlogged camps, the monotony and boredom, the poor scant rations and decided to go and be comfortable during a period marked by military inaction. This latter group was by far the largest and most of them would return to the colors in the spring but their voluntary absence was "detrimental to good order and military discipline." Apparently a great many officers sympathized with the men because furloughs were granted widely and units were sent on detached duty to places near their homes.

By the end of January 1863, both army Commander Bragg and Department Commander Johnston were moved to take action. Johnston tried to end both furloughs and sick leave because so many men were using these means to go home that the army was being drained. Johnston wanted all sick men sent to division hospitals where a regular check would be made on both their physical condition and their presence. It appeared to "Old Joe" that a soldier was likely to recover a lot faster in a hospital under the cold eye of an army doctor than he would if in the loving arms of his family. Bragg issued a stern order that all commissioned officers not disabled, or with written orders placing them on detached duty, were to report to Tullahoma within 20 days, or be dismissed in disgrace. General Order #23 notes that an examination of muster rolls showed "several thousand" officers and men absent with furloughs, and orders for detached service. Authority for furloughs and detached service was henceforth limited to army headquarters. For some men, these restrictions came too late. They were gone, never to return. Private John Hudson got a furlough from General Buford while encamped near Beech Grove. Hudson intended to slip through Union lines back to Kentucky. In order to help finance his trip he offered to carry letters to the folks at home for $5 per letter. He would also bring letters back for the same rate. This mail never got through because Hudson was captured in Gallatin County, Kentucky, and sent to Camp Chase.[56]

Having brandished a stick, Bragg then dangled a carrot; he, like Rosecrans, tried to boost morale. The commanding general authorized units which had fought there to put the word "Murfreesboro" on their battle flags. In addition, officers were to recommend subordinates for promotion, and regiments were to select, by vote, one noncommissioned officer and one private who were to receive a medal for valor.[57]

Another source of strength were the numerous men who had come under the conscription law enacted by the Confederate Congress the preceding year. During much of the summer and fall of 1862 the Army of Tennessee had been absent from the state or too busy to sweep up these men. Now, however, the Confederates had a tenuous hold on a good part of the state, thanks to their cavalry force, and it was an opportune time to bring in the harvest of manpower. General Johnston and Governor Isham Harris appointed Brigadier General Gideon Pillow to head a bureau to bring in both conscripts and volunteers, place them in camps, and begin the process of training. Pillow had disgraced himself at Fort Donelson less than a year before but he found his place as head of this bureau. With headquarters at Columbia, Pillow was in position to reach both west and north of the Confederate cavalry cordon to pull in men. Although periodic Union forays from Franklin, Tennessee, caused him to move around a bit he would often report that he was forwarding "another lot of volunteers." As numbers in the ranks shrank, units were merged, and officers left without commands as a result were sent to Pillow to help in recruiting and in training. It is estimated that by the time the Tullahoma campaign closed down his operation Pillow had added 10,000 men to army ranks.

Some of these men were absent without leave and were brought back in by cavalry patrols under Pillow's general supervision. Bragg must have needed the manpower badly, for although he had the men court-martialed as deserters the sentences were quite light. On January 17, 1863, Private Eli Cothran, Co. H, 48th Tennessee Infantry, left his command and went to his home in Lawrence County, about 85 miles west of Tullahoma. On March 1, Private Cothran was arrested by the cavalry and sent to Tullahoma. At his court-martial on March 23 Cothran was sentenced to three months' hard labor "on government works" and loss of pay. Since Bragg usually shot deserters this was lenient treatment indeed. Several deserters shared Cothran's punishment but the lengthy court session at Tullahoma sentenced only six men to be shot.[58]

While the cavalry was of great importance to the Army of Tennessee the freer lifestyle, the mobility, the opportunity for small unit action attracted a number of "Buttermilk Rangers," men who had joined the cavalry but who had become mere roaming marauders. Cavalry commanders were ordered to dismount and to send to the guardhouse all men absent without permission and those who constantly avoided duty.[59]

As was the case on the other side of the lines, the Confederates found the contributions of army employees to be valuable because they freed trained soldiers to return to the fighting lines, and, as in Rosecran's case, many of these Confederate army employees were Black. General Order #39 required that "proper medical attention will be given to all employees of this army, black as well as white, and suitable accommodations will immediately be provided for them."[60] The number of Black employees is not disclosed in the available records but the fact that a general order was issued suggests that the number was rather large. It is also noteworthy that this order placed Black and White employees on an equal footing as to medical care, rations, and housing. And, since this was the case, it is also clear that these Black employees were not the "body servants" of a few upper-class individuals; they were men employed by the army whose service was considered a valuable contribution to the Confederate war effort.

In an attempt to make sure no potential fighting men had been overlooked Bragg and Johnston took a look at supply services far behind the lines. What they found in the Quartermaster Department tells quite a tale about the South's manpower condition at the midpoint of the war. In Atlanta the Quartermaster's Department employed more than three thousand people manufacturing uniforms for the army. Of these, 27 were men, with the rest women.[61]

By May 10, as the campaigning season opened, Bragg had reached his apex. His cavalry screen, and his conscript bureau, his strict orders had brought his army to a total of 52,855 effectives.[62] A month later, just as the Tullahoma campaign was about to open, Bragg reported 46,260 effectives. Of this number 653 were in the artillery, and 12,703 were cavalry. The artillery number does not represent enough men to serve 124 guns but Bragg counted only trained artillerymen; the gun crews were fleshed out with infantry soldiers drafted for less skilled roles. This left Polk and Hardee with 29,862 infantry divided equally between them. Breckenridge and McCown's infantry, along with Van Dorn's cavalry, had been sent off to Pemberton at Vicksburg; Morgan went riding off on a mad mission across the Ohio, depriving Bragg of another two thousand cavalry while Colonel Philip D. Roddey was sent to protect northwestern Alabama as best he could with 1,600 troopers.[63] After six months of strenuous effort Bragg was not much stronger than he had been on the retreat from Murfreesboro.

Soldiers must be armed as well as mustered and fed and both army commanders spent a good deal of time during the 1863 winter months trying to get weapons for their men. One of the stereotypes of the war is that of a struggle between the industrial North and the agricultural South. The quest for arms shows this stereotype is based on truth.

Rosecrans' primary concern was to build up his mounted arm, so most of his quest for weapons centered on cavalry equipment. As early as the end of January, while he was calling for more horses, the general asked for 2,500 revolving rifles and breech-loading carbines to arm his cavalry. Two thoughts seem to be in Rosecrans' head at once: he wanted more cavalry but was not sure he could get enough, so he wanted to compensate for numbers with firepower. Of course, such weapons as he wanted were expensive, needed special ammunition which complicated supply problems, and were thought to encourage soldiers to waste ammunition since they could fire so quickly. Not surprisingly, Rosecrans and Halleck argued over this request at length.[64] Rosecrans took his case to Secretary of War Edwin Stanton and would, no doubt, have gone to President Lincoln had he not gotten his way. In February, word arrived in Murfreesboro that 2,483 Burnside carbines were being shipped but other breech loaders could be shipped if he wanted. Only 300 revolving rifles were manufactured by the Colt Arms Company each month, but the Army of the Cumberland would get all of them.[65]

By mid-March Rosecrans had received the arms he had asked for or they were en route. Between the supplies at Louisville and Nashville the cavalry had access to 3,976 breech-loading weapons and 485 revolving rifles. Before the end of the month he wrote Stanton asking for 5,000 Sharps' carbines, .54 caliber. From 2,500 arms of the latest pattern Rosecrans had increased his demands to 10,000. Less than a week after asking for the Sharps' carbines Rosecrans was told the following were being shipped to Nashville: 150 Sharps' carbines, 1,400 Gallaghers, 226 Smiths, and 500 Burnsides for a total of 2,276 weapons. Encouraged by success the general promptly requested 6,000 of the new pattern of Colt's pistols, getting them as well. It was at this same time that Christopher Spencer arrived in the camps of the Army of the Cumberland selling his famous rifle to Wilder's Brigade.[66] Rosecrans was going to have well-armed mounted men.

John Wilder, born in New York, had worked in a foundry at Columbus, Ohio, and understood many of the technical points of designing and manufacturing machinery. When the war began he was building hydraulic machinery in Greensburg, Indiana, and held several patents for his designs. He was so anxious for his men to have the seven-shot repeaters he took out a loan from his hometown bank to purchase them and his men signed notes to repay the colonel on the installment plan, a little each pay day. About the time Wilder purchased the Spencers he received permission to mount his brigade on horses impressed from the countryside. Soon, Wilder's men had become one of the few units in the Army of the Cumberland which could operate rapidly over a wide range, not supported by infantry, and still attack or defend itself.[67]

After the first of April there were no more large requests for weapons. It is very significant that Rosecrans never did clamor for artillery or infantry arms. He felt he was well equipped with these and an adequate supply for replacements appeared to arrive regularly.

From the time the Confederates moved into the Tullahoma lines they were short of guns and ammunition. In a report to Richmond, Colonel Preston Johnston had claimed that on March 15 "This army is in a high state of efficency, well clad and armed . . ."[68] The evidence shows the colonel was wearing very rosy glasses indeed. Shortages of ammunition were so critical that units coming off guard duty were ordered to stop the common practice of firing their guns to clear the loads. Instead, the just relieved guards were to draw the powder and shot and turn it over to the regimental ordnance sergeant. As this supply accumulated the sergeant would draw cartridge paper and roll new rounds.[69]

January also found the artillery to be weak, a problem that was not rectified when active campaigning began in June. McCown's Division was ordered to reorganize its batteries so there would be four guns in each unit. The makeup of these batteries is significant because two of them would have 12-pounder Napoleon guns, one would have rifled weapons, but two would have obsolescent 6 pounders.[70] In all, the artillery could count only 64 guns in the various camps in February, although an additional four batteries were being organized and this would bring the total to 80 pieces.[71] These batteries were not as well organized as they needed to be; however, because Hardee reported he had no field grade artillery officers and, thus, there was no coordination of effort. Each infantry division commander controlled his guns but there was no unified command which could mass guns at strategic points. This need was remedied in April when Llewellyn Hoxton was promoted to major and made chief of artillery in Hardee's corps.[72]

As spring came Bragg had managed to increase his artillery strength to double what it had been in February; at least he had assembled 125 guns. He still was weak in weight of metal. Of his total number 80 were 6-pounder and 12-pounder howitzers while another 16 were 12-pounder Napoleons. Only 29 pieces were rifles including one Ellsworth breech loader.[73] Not all these guns would be available when Rosecrans moved forward since three batteries would be sent to Mississippi. Another trouble was the condition of the horses needed to move the guns. The quantity and quality of Southern horseflesh was steadily declining and, as the campaign opened, the Army of Tennessee had a severe shortage of draft animals. Hardee said he could hardly move forward or backward.[74]

Infantry and cavalry soldiers were no better off for weapons. In early February most brigades had a number of men who had no weapons. On February 11 Bragg ordered his brigadiers to arm their men with whatever weapons were at hand but he hoped to issue improved weapons as they became available. To help make them available General Johnston wrote Secretary of War James Seddon that Bragg would need 10,000 rifles within a month and asked the secretary to make heroic efforts to provide them. Seddon replied that there were no spare rifles in the Confederacy although the government did own some in Bermuda and he would dispatch a blockade runner to get them.[75] While Rosecrans received 10,000 breech loaders, revolving rifles, and repeaters the Confederacy sent a blockade runner to Bermuda in the hopes of bringing into the country a few hundred muzzle loaders. The campaign was being fought in middle Tennessee, but it was being won in Connecticut and Massachusetts.

By the middle of March the situation had not improved. Repair shops in Chattanooga had sent forward 1,450 rifles which had been gleaned from the battlefield at Murfreesboro and had been repaired. The workshops told Bragg that all weapons which could be readily repaired had been delivered, and as the repairs became more difficult the number they could deliver with any dependability would probably be about eight hundred per month.[76]

The Army of Tennessee depended on its cavalry to protect its food-producing area, but the ability of the horse soldiers to perform this function was limited by their lack of weapons. From Columbia, Forrest reported that as of February 19, 1863 he commanded three thousand men but he was short some six hundred guns. He had been told there were eight hundred carbines at Chattanooga but they all needed repair. About the same time, General Polk told army headquarters that Colonel A. A. Russell had just reported to him as ordered with his cavalry command of seven hundred men; unfortunately, four hundred of this number were unarmed. As he moved north along the cavalry line, posting his men, General John Wharton reported leaving the 3rd Georgia Cavalry at Beech Grove along with Major Zacharia Thomason's Battalion "which will be armed in a few days."[77] Beech Grove was near the mouth of Hoover's Gap on the best and most direct road from Rosecran's army to Bragg's right flank. Unarmed men were left to guard this road.

The same report which tallied Bragg's artillery collection also chronicled the arms carried by his infantry and cavalry. Of the approximately 32,000 infantry in the ranks not quite 20,000 had rifles, the rest had smoothbores. Among the cavalry fewer than 1,500 had carbines while about 4,700 had long-barreled rifles. Some 753 carried shotguns. Only 1,566 Rebel horsemen had a revolver while 42 carried single shot pistols.[78] This is fewer than 8,000 weapons of all sorts for 12,000 troopers. The very weak weaponry, possessed by the Confederate cavalry, helps to account for the successful saber charges mounted by some elements of the Union cavalry during the Tullahoma campaign.

With food scarce, manpower short, and weapons in scant supply Bragg tried to compensate by fortifying various points along his line. On January 26 Hardee sent Bragg his engineer officers, Captain J. W. Green and Lieutenant George M. Helm, to learn where the commander wanted fortifications built around Tullahoma. Hardee thought none were needed since the position could easily be turned by the Manchester-Decherd-Winchester road and, besides, there were no terrain features which gave the town defensible flanks. There were "no advantages in this position which can compensate for superior numbers," Old Reliable concluded. But Bragg wanted the dirt to fly and so it did. A month later General Johnston called the results a "slight" fortification and soon after Colonel Preston Johnston would report that "the fortifications are a line of slight redoubts extending in an arc from the Fayetteville to the Manchester road and not flanked by rifle pits. There is an abatis of felled timber 1,500 feet wide and four miles long. These works are too weak to rely on and too strong to abandon." The best position at Tullahoma was an earthwork capable of holding a garrison of five hundred men, named Fort Rains in honor of Brigadier James E. Rains who has been killed at Murfreesboro. General H. D. Clanton described the fort in a letter to his wife. "It is 125 yards across. The ditch is twelve feet wide and eight deep and the dirt makes a wall eight feet high, and has twelve cannon in it. We have cut down the trees on one thousand acres of thick woodland.[79] At any rate, these fortifications were never finished and no fighting occurred at Tullahoma.

The same fate awaited the more extensive works Polk constructed at Shelbyville. From Guys Gap, four miles north of the town to an inner line about a mile from town, the Army of Tennessee built its first earthworks since Corinth in the spring of 1862.

And in the end, as at Corinth, they would go away without defending them.

The situation for 1863 was set. Rosecrans needed to fight and win for political as well as military reasons. Bragg needed to show he could win if any confidence was to be regained from his subordinate commanders but the supply and manpower situation was weighted against Bragg. Both men would have to evaluate the setting for the coming campaign and see what they could accomplish.

Chapter Two
The Setting

As Rosecrans looked at his maps he must have furrowed his brow with puzzlement. There were a lot of roads which could be used to accomplish his goal of eventually reaching Chattanooga. He would have to dominate those roads and deceive his opponent, but the physical resources he needed were there. Most of the roads were not hard surfaced which meant they would make for slow going during the winter months, but when spring came and the roads dried there would be plenty of opportunity for maneuver.

Farthest to the west, two roads from Nashville converged at Franklin and, from there, a good road led to Spring Hill and Columbia. This road gave Rosecrans a route which approached the extreme left flank of Bragg's cavalry line, a route which would allow the Union-mounted troops to challenge Confederate control of the food and forage rich areas of western middle Tennessee.

Another pike ran from Nashville to Nolensville and then to Triune. Below Triune this road forked with the left branch trending eastward through Eagleville, Rover, Unionville, and so to Shelbyville while the right branch ran south to Lewisburg in Bragg's food collecting area.

In December, when he marched out to battle at Stones River, Rosecrans had followed the Murfreesboro Pike. This road paralleled the Nashville and Chattanooga (N&C) Railroad and was now the major supply link for the Army of the Cumberland back to Nashville and, beyond, to Louisville. However, from Murfreesboro a good road ran west linking with Triune and Franklin. Thus, Rosecrans had two good cavalry posts to his west at Triune and Franklin and they had firm links with army headquarters at Murfreesboro and back to the supply base at Nashville.

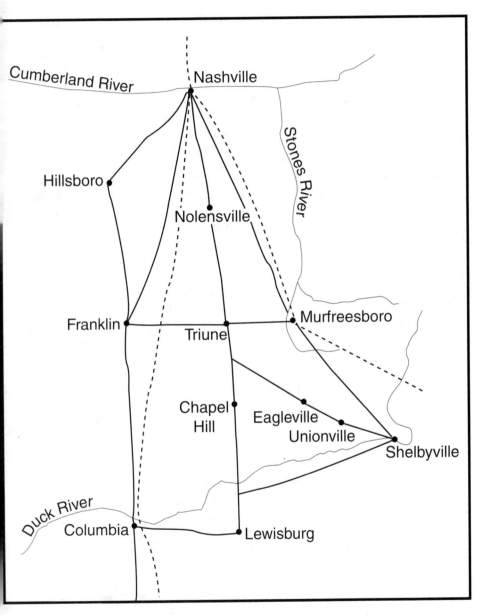

Road Network around Nashville, Tennessee, 1863

Map drawn by author

From Murfreesboro another network of roads spread in a fan from southwest to north of east. The best road ran south through Fosterville and Christiana, passed through Guys Gap, and entered Shelbyville. Several tracks linked this pike with the Eagleville-Rover-Unionville area to the west. To the east of the Shelbyville road another pike paralleled the N&C Railroad, passing through the Liberty Gap area to reach Bell Buckle, Wartrace, and Tullahoma. Not far north of that route, the Manchester Pike used Hoover's Gap to reach the county seat of Coffee County and then sent out other roads to touch Tullahoma or to cross Elk River. If Rosecrans wanted to use it, another road led east from Murfreesboro to Bradyville, Woodbury, and McMinnville. This last town was the right flank of Bragg's cavalry line and was linked to Tullahoma by a spur line of the N&C which ran through Manchester before reaching the main line at Tullahoma. From both Bradyville and Woodbury roads ran south to connect with the Manchester Pike.

Lots of roads were available to Rosecrans. If his mounted troops used their numbers and superior weapons properly, he could bemuse Bragg in one direction while turning his other flank.

Like Rosecrans, as Bragg sat in his Tullahoma headquarters looking at his maps he must have furrowed his brow with puzzlement. There were a lot of roads and, to achieve his purpose, he had to defend them all. Defense was a high priority in Bragg's mind; he had no intention of taking the offensive unless Rosecrans retreated or was weakened by sending large reinforcements to Grant.

From the left flank of his cavalry screen at Columbia there were no good, direct roads running towards his infantry position. All communication had to funnel towards Lewisburg before moving further east. This presented a double problem. If the Columbia flank was attacked, it would be difficult to reinforce, and the link via Lewisburg was vulnerable to Union forces at Triune. Once past Lewisburg the route to Shelbyville and Tullahoma was safe.

Bragg had placed his foot soldiers along the rugged Highland Rim with his infantry left at Shelbyville and his right at Beech Grove, a village near the eastern end of Hoover's Gap. A railroad spur ran from Shelbyville to Wartrace parallel to the Fairfield Road and the pike ran on to Beech Grove. At Wartrace the branch railroad met the main N&C line which Bragg could use back to his headquarters at Tullahoma and Chattanooga. Two roads from Shelbyville to Tullahoma completed the Shelbyville-Wartrace-Tullahoma triangle.

From Shelbyville one road led west to Unionville and a cavalry outpost at Rover. From Rover pickets were stretched cross-country toward Columbia via College Grove and Chapel Hill and also forward toward Eagleville and Triune. Another road ran basically north

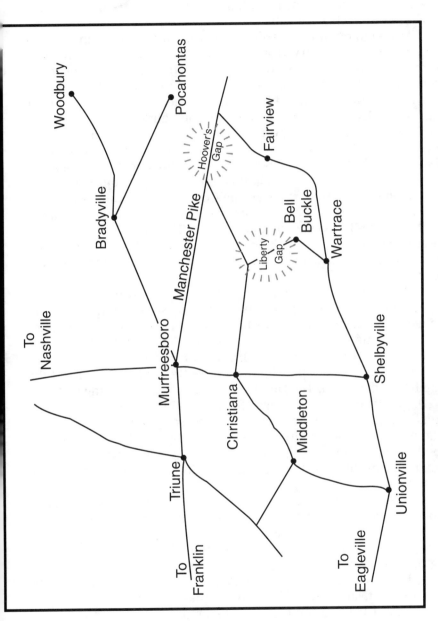

Road Network around Murfreesboro, Tennessee, 1863

Map drawn by author

from Shelbyville to Murfreesboro and Rosecrans' army. Bragg placed Polk in Shelbyville and ordered him to fortify Guys Gap on this last road to hold back Rosecrans.

Although many of his troops spent the winter in camps around Tullahoma, the infantry front from Wartrace to Beech Grove was commanded by General Hardee. "Old Reliable" had two poor roads from the Fairfield and Wartrace area back towards Tullahoma but he could follow the railroad once he reached Wartrace. The major road in Hardee's sector was on his extreme right flank, the Manchester Pike. After leaving Hoover's Gap this road crossed the Garrison Fork of Duck River and traversed Matts Hollow before arriving at Manchester. From the courthouse in this county seat village a short distance southeast was the Elk River and the N&C Railroad.

Beginning at Hoover's Gap the Confederate cavalry spread an arc north and east to cover country roads which connected with the Murfreesboro-Bradyville-Woodbury road. This arc, commanded by Joseph Wheeler, included the command of John Hunt Morgan who occupied the northeast anchor point at McMinnville on the railroad spur back to Tullahoma.

The country guarded by the western cavalry wing was of more immediate value to Bragg because it was the source of his food and forage. The country guarded by his northeastern wing was of greater strategic value since Rosecrans could use it to cut behind Bragg's right and block off his infantry from Chattanooga.

The major geographic features were the Highland Rim and the Cumberland Plateau. The Highland Rim is not a single ridge but is a ragged plateau, the edge of which stands 600 to 800 feet above the Cumberland Basin and the eastern Tennessee Valley in which Nashville and Chattanooga are located. The edge of the rim provided good defensive terrain, but the left of Bragg's infantry was off the rim at Shelbyville and his line was very long for the infantry force on hand.

Once the rim is reached, the country becomes flat with slow-moving streams, a sandy topsoil with underlying clay makes for bottomless mire in wet weather and lots of dust in dry, the whole being covered with dense thickets of scrub black oak. Pioneers looking for good land moved right on by much of this area which they named the Oak Barrens. This flat area is from 20 to 30 miles wide, east to west, and ends abruptly in the east at the foot of the Cumberland Plateau. Actually, in the area of the Tullahoma campaign the plateau is not a plateau at all, but a series of rugged, flat-topped mountain ridges which rise from 500 to 900 feet above the Highland Rim and fill the country from Cowan to Chattanooga. While these ridges would have made good defensive positions the area was bare of food and empty of roads, making the supply problem impossible to solve.

Bragg would have to make his stand pretty much where he was along the Highland Rim else he would lose the area from which he gathered his supplies. Rosecrans had to decide whether to fight in the position chosen by Bragg or to try to maneuver him into a position easier to get at—or, perhaps, maneuver him out of middle Tennessee entirely. It would depend on who controlled the roads. Cavalry fights began early in 1863 as the Confederates tried to make worse the Union supply problems and Rosecrans tried to build up his mounted force.

The star of Bedford Forrest was just rising and, during the opening phase of the campaign, he was placed under the orders of 26-year-old Major General Joseph Wheeler who was put in command of all Confederate cavalry in middle Tennessee.[1] This matter of age did not sit well with Forrest nor did Wheeler's "West Point" ways, but the two did give Rosecrans some reason to worry. On January 10 these two moved their force, without opposition, to Harpeth Shoals on the Cumberland River and captured three transports plus a gunboat. The major enemy on this expedition was the weather since there was a lot of sleet and snow.[2] Soon after, Bragg decided to hit the river line again and sent Wheeler, with Forrest under his command, to attack the village of Dover where Fort Donelson is located. Forrest saw no need to make this expedition, much less any need to attack the Union position. His men were short on ammunition and food and, even if they took the fort, they could not hold it. The whole thing looked to be a very costly temporary break in Rosecrans' river supply line. At the Cumberland Iron Works, nine miles outside Dover, two companies of Yankees were attacked. Most were captured but some escaped to warn the garrison of the fort, making Forrest sure the attack had little chance. However, when the time came Forrest led one charge on horseback and another on foot but neither made much headway against the defenders. Running out of ammunition, the Confederates fell back. In their bivouac that night Forrest blamed Wheeler for the loss of life and told him, to his face, he would never serve under him again.[3] Rosecrans thought this failed attack might lead to the capture of the Confederate force, but the Rebel horsemen made it back to friendly territory without difficulty.

Rosecrans did find one weak spot in the Confederate cavalry screen, a weak spot he would worry continuously until it became a key part of his campaign. On January 30 Rosecrans ordered J. C. Davis to move past Nolensville, secure Triune, and advance on the Eagleville-Unionville road. Even if this move did not catch the

Major General Joseph Wheeler

"Fightin' Joe" didn't do well at Shelbyville.

Wheeler-Forrest command returning from Dover it would secure the right flank of Rosecrans' line.[4] In this sector Wheeler had Wither's Division, headquartered in Shelbyville, but covering the area from Unionville back east and northeast to Guys Gap. Colonel W. B. Wade had his regiment at Unionville with an outpost at Rover. Colonel Roddey was ordered to bring his command up from northern Alabama to Columbia and picket the Duck River towards Unionville to provide a link between Withers at Shelbyville and Forrest who had returned to Columbia.[5] Roddey had seen much service in northern Alabama but his men were not fully armed and were totally unacquainted with the country they were to picket. Roddey was more accustomed to functioning as an independent commander who raided and tried to defend his territory against small Union attacks and foraging parties. He had to learn how to perform the task of working with a major army to provide information and to serve as a part of a larger cavalry screen. Though he made it obvious he was willing to learn, Roddey appeared often in reports in a negative light. In April he would be ordered back to northern Alabama to do the kind of work he did well but during his time in Tennessee his sector of the lines were viewed as a weak spot and Rosecrans probed the area frequently.

The problem of how to deal with Forrest's refusal to serve under Wheeler was solved when Earl Van Dorn arrived from Mississippi with almost five thousand cavalry. This increase in strength allowed Bragg to organize his troopers into two corps, one under Wheeler which would guard the right wing, and one under Van Dorn which would protect the left. Forrest would be under Van Dorn.[6]

By this time blue-clad horsemen were on the move again. From Columbia, Gid Pillow reported that Franklin had been occupied by Yankees and that the bridge over the Harpeth River was being rebuilt. Not faraway, U.S. forces foraged around Millersburg and were reported to be taking everything, declaring they would live off the country since their line of supply north had been interrupted. Colonel W. B. Wade, commanding Confederate forces at Unionville, reported that armed and uniformed Negroes were in the U.S. forces.[7] At this stage in the war these were probably teamsters who had been issued some military clothing and who had acquired arms to defend themselves and the wagons they drove.

Both armies were active in the east as well as their western fronts. On March 1 Lieutenant Colonel James Bowles led the 2nd Kentucky of Morgan's command on a reconnaissance towards Bradyville. Along the way he was attacked by the 4th Ohio and the Kentucky troopers had to cut their way back towards Woodbury, part of the time fighting hand-to-hand. Sergeant Tom Boss, one of the 2nd Kentucky, killed one opponent with an axe.[8] This area would prove to be the most vulnerable in all of Bragg's extended line and this vulnerability, along with the strategic value of the area, would draw the main blow Rosecrans would strike in June. The vulnerability was increased by the decline in efficiency of John Morgan and his men.

The year 1862 had been good to Morgan. He had won victories, fame, and a bride; some said the latter had made him soft, stolen his heart away from his men. It is quite true that Morgan stayed with "Miss Mattie" in a fine house in McMinnville while his men inhabited makeshift shelters at Woodbury, Liberty, and other points 25 miles closer to the enemy. No matter how loyal they might be to their chief some resentment was bound to grow in the hearts of his men. Not just morale, but materiel suffered as well. One visitor to a bivouac of Morgan's men reported them armed with several different types of shotguns and rifles, "all sorts of saddles, some with rope stirrups, many of the saddles without blankets, all sorts of bridles, in fact a conglomerate get up, fairly laughable."[9] And all the while Rosecrans was ordering breech loaders and repeaters. The halo of glory was fading around Morgan, and his men would have to face an enemy increasingly more numerous, better mounted, and better armed.

The same week as the Bradyville skirmish the action bounced back to the western end of the lines. Van Dorn got word from scouts that a large Union force was advancing on Columbia along the Franklin Pike and its parallel Nashville & Decatur Railroad. He decided to challenge this force at Thompson's Station where the pike and railroad ran through a deep valley. Early on the morning of March 5 Van Dorn was in position just south of the station. Three brigades of cavalry were dismounted and strung across the valley while Forrest's command was placed well out on the right, still on their horses. The Union force of five regiments of infantry with some artillery and about six hundred cavalry was commanded by Colonel John Coburn. Having advanced slowly, he was just about ready to retire in the face of what he deemed superior force when he bumped into the Southern battleline.

A short but sharp artillery exchange convinced the Union horse and guns to head back to Franklin without standing on ceremony, but the infantry could not move fast enough. Van Dorn charged, dismounted, and though repulsed came back twice more, pinning Coburn in place. Forrest, who was well out on the flank, rode around Coburn's left, dismounted his men, and rolled up the Yankee line. Coburn and more than 1,200 of his men surrendered.[10] The engagement of Thompson's Station was a great public relations coup for

Forrest. His men had done most of the fighting and they also got most of the credit for the victory. The glowing report of Forrest's performance printed in the Chattanooga *Rebel* weakened the ties between Van Dorn, a vain man, and Forrest.

Colonel Coburn had not been sent out into no-man's-land alone. Rosecrans had ordered General Philip R. Sheridan and General James Steedman to probe towards Lewisburg along the Chapel Hill Road. As this force drove back the gray troopers of Colonel Roddey, Bragg reacted by ordering General Patton Anderson to send one infantry brigade from Shelbyville towards Unionville to reinforce the cavalry unit at that place. Anderson was then told to take Deas' Brigade and advance against the Union forces at Chapel Hill.[11] Sheridan and Steedman didn't like the look of the country or the sound of the fight behind their right shoulders at Thompson's Station, so they soon went back where they had come from. All of this produced a great deal of excitement and would have raised clouds of dust had the weather been dry, but nothing like the fight at Thompson's Station took place, although Bragg was once again made to feel sensitive about the Eagleville-Rover-Unionville sector of his cavalry line. To further shore up this area a cavalry post was established at the village of Middleton in an attempt to link Unionville, which was west of Shelbyville, with Fosterville, which was north of Shelbyville. This new position would seal a gap in the Confederate screen[12] but this little outpost was soon in the middle of almost daily brushes between cavalry patrols and probes of the opposing lines.

Having probed to the west, Rosecrans now punched to the east. It looked to "Old Rosy" that Morgan was vulnerable and he sent a force out to do battle with him. This unit, commanded by Colonel A. S. Hall, moved out the Milton Road on March 19 and, finding Morgan in the vicinity, took defensive positions on a cedar-covered hill. Most of the Union troops were infantry, and some of the mounted troops were carrying the new Spencer repeaters. All in all, lightly armed, dismounted cavalry had no business attacking such a force in such a place, but Morgan did just that and fought for about an hour. At the end of that time he had lost almost fifteen percent of the force engaged while the Union losses were slight.[13] This was the first setback Morgan had received and it reinforced a growing perception that he had lost his edge as a combat commander. Clearly, his command had declined in efficiency just at the time the Union forces were becoming stronger and such a weakness would act as a lightning rod for other Union strikes. Doubts were also growing on his own side of the lines. Wheeler did not seem able to control Morgan and Bragg was convinced he had been promoted above his capacity; Morgan should have stayed a brigadier.[14]

The Union success in holding down Morgan was soon over-shadowed in many minds by Forrest erupting on the scene again. On the night of March 24 Forrest took parts of two brigades and penetrated the Union cavalry screen at Franklin in order to attack two groups of Yankees at Brentwood and at the nearby railroad bridge over the little Harpeth River. Guided by his usual philosophy of "Keep the skeer on 'em" Forrest had chosen to attack the survivors of the Thompson's Station engagement. The Union commander, Colonel Bloodgood, at first refused to surrender but when he saw artillery going into position he changed his mind. Shortly after, three hundred Michigan infantry surrendered their stockade at the railroad bridge. For a time, the hunter became the hunted when Union cavalry under Brigadier General Green C. Smith hit Forrest's rear guard and wagon train with some seven hundred troopers. This force must have seemed larger than it was since the men were armed with Burnside carbines and a few had repeaters. Soon Forrest himself was on the scene making the air smoke with "cussin'" and either the volume of his profanity or the dismounted charge he led sent the Union forces back where they had come from, but not before they drove off or killed the mules hitched to the captured wagons. Minus the now stationary vehicles but with a command largely rearmed, courtesy of the U.S. government, Forrest left the field. "Old Bed" may have been aided by information just passed along by General John Wharton. A guide, Lycurgus House, had been sent from the 1st Tennessee Infantry to guide Lieutenant William Smith of the Texas Rangers and three other men to the house of General William H. Smith on the Wilkinson Pike, only three miles out of Murfreesboro. This party had returned to report no major movement taking place at the main Union base.[15]

If the western area was not too fruitful for Rosecrans, the eastern area was. Like a shark sensing blood in the water Rosecrans again went after Morgan. Brigadier General David Stanley's blue cavalry, accompanied by an infantry force of 1,500, marched toward Liberty. Colonel Richard Gano, senior Confederate in the area, took up a defensive position on Snow Hill on April 3. This would have been a good position had there been any defensive works or natural cover, but the slopes were rather bare. When the Union artillery opened fire the Johnnies began to back up while the Yankee cavalry turned their left flank. In the face of an infantry attack Gano wisely pulled out but his command got rather scattered, staying that way for several days.

Such successes began to lead to unusual proposals about thwarting the Union effort. Lieutenant Colonel J. C. Malone, Jr., of the 14th Alabama Cavalry, asked the advice of General Polk about

the propriety of capturing Rosecrans. Polk approved the idea, especially if the papers of the Yankee adjutant general could be taken at
the same time. However, Polk added, killing Rosecrans would be
"uncivilized" despite Yankee atrocities. Colonel Malone replied he
would kill Rosecrans only if the general put up a fight. Apparently
no other action was ever taken on this daring concept.[16]

Success over Morgan was heady stuff and the Union boys loved
it. For the last two years it had only been Southern boys singing "If
you want to have a good time, jine th' cavalry" but now Yanks thought
they could have fun, too. Specifically, they thought they could make
cavalry raids like the big boys did, so Colonel Abel Streight convinced the Union high command to let him try. His attempt led to
one of Bedford Forrest's greatest triumphs and cost Rosecrans a
brigade of cavalry, but the details of that episode took place far
outside the area of the Tullahoma campaign.[17]

Reinforcing success, Rosecrans gave General Joseph Reynolds
a mixed command of 6,600 men and sent them off towards
McMinnville. Knowing Morgan's command was scattered at several
outposts and picket points, Reynolds wanted to slip through the
gray cordon, take McMinnville, destroy military property, and kill or
capture Morgan. Early on the morning of April 19 Reynolds slipped
through Morgan's lines and soon had various outpost commanders
guessing about what he intended. Morgan had only about 40 men at
McMinnville when Reynolds swarmed into the town. Fortunately,
Morgan was mounted and on the street when the Union eruption
occurred and dashed out of town. Also fortunate was the devotion
of one of his men who charged the blue column head-on, two pistols blazing, in the stereotype of the "hell for leather" Rebel cavalry-
man. Yet another clever and devoted Johnnie Reb pretended to be
Morgan and surrendered. The Yanks were so pleased with their catch
they quit the pursuit of the real thing to take the bogus general back
to headquarters. A cotton weaving factory, the railroad depot, two
railroad trestles, and 30,000 pounds of bacon were destroyed in
what the Chattanooga *Rebel* called "an ugly business."[18] Bragg very
sharply told Wheeler to tighten up his command and to cordon the
right flank more effectively else a Yankee thrust would go through
that area to Bridgeport and destroy the railroad bridge over the Tennessee, severing Bragg from Chattanooga and northern Alabama.[19]
It was under the sting of these blows that Morgan began to ponder
redeeming himself with another spectacular raid, this one across
the Ohio.

As a part of the increased activity in the area, Colonel James
Thompson, stationed at Hoover's Gap, reported that on April 22 a
U.S. push had penetrated all the way to Beech Grove. This force was

accompanied by artillery which shelled the colonel's position quite heavily. In response, the brigades of Brigadier General Ben Hardin Helm and Brigadier General John Calvin Brown were ordered from Manchester to Beech Grove.[20] On this expedition Rosecrans probably received news of a discovery which would guide much of his later strategic thinking. There were no extensive earthworks in the gap, and the bridge across the creek was solid enough to carry the trains of a large part of his army. The Manchester Pike, which led past Bragg's right flank, was a practicable route to the Confederate rear.

As the month of May opened the initiative was passing to the Union cavalry. The horses and weapons which Rosecrans had gathered were being used by men steadily gaining experience in using their equipment and increasingly confident in themselves. Shortages of horses and weapons were eroding the Confederate competitive edge and, worst of all, the Confederate command structure was falling apart. The capture of Streight's raiders in early May would be the last big Confederate cavalry success of the Tullahoma campaign.

By the time Forrest returned from Rome, Georgia, where he had taken his prisoners, he was in command of all cavalry on the Confederate left. Van Dorn had gone into dangerous territory once too often and had paid the price. This territory was not occupied by the Yankees, it was occupied by another man's wife. On May 7 a justly jealous husband made sure the general would never again unsheath his sword. Wheeler proved incapable of making long-range plans, could not control Morgan, and was ineffective in breaking Rosecrans' supply line. As to Morgan, his men were drifting away, many of them into the mountains of southern Kentucky, where they had hopes of getting good horses and were closer to family and friends. To complete this breakdown, Forrest was shot on June 13 by one of his artillery officers and so was out of the command picture during the crucial opening days of the campaign.

By the time Rosecrans made his first move toward the Elk River all of Van Dorn's men had been sent back to Mississippi and Roddey had been dispatched to northern Alabama. Bragg was seeing his cavalry command structure crumble and his troopers decline in number from 16,000 to about 9,000. Looking back at this situation many years later, General Arthur Manigault would reflect on the failure of the Confederate cavalry. "At Tullahoma it appeared to be the intention of our General to receive the attack of the enemy, should he decide to make one, and after finding out it was not their intention to do so, as it turned out he had time to place himself across the path of the Federal Commander, and force him either to fight or to retire. This he did not do. Why, I do not know, but can only conjecture that he did not regard himself as sufficiently strong to resist, and that success was too doubtful under the circumstances to render a battle advisable or prudent, or that owing to the inferiority of our Cavalry, or their inability or failure to furnish him information; he remained in ignorance of the enemies movements or plans, until it was too late to check or prevent them or to take such steps as under other circumstances and with more general information he would have done. It often appeared to me that many of our failures or misfortunes arose from our lamentable deficiency in this branch of the service."[21]

Rosecrans exercised his growing cavalry initiative by increasing his patrols and foraging expeditions. On May 2 General Steedman reported he had led a foraging train east of Stones River toward Alexandria and Lebanon, country once controlled by Morgan. Not only was Steedman successful in bringing back food, he had a handful of prisoners, but more importantly, he had met no opposition.[22]

From Triune and Franklin regular patrols and probes were sent down the various pikes toward Spring Hill, Chapel Hill, Lewisburg, Eagleville, and Unionville. Usually these resulted in men of both sides doing little more than warily watching each other, sometimes the blue riders came home with modest trophies of men or material, and sometimes they came flying home with Johnnie Rebs yipping at their coattails. The significant thing is that the Northern troops were so often on the offensive.

On May 21 Rosecrans sent out a double offensive probe. Wilder was sent from Murfreesboro out the Liberty Pike with the goal of reaching the gap on that road. There, he was to turn northeast to the Manchester Pike at Hoover's Gap. This was purely a scouting mission and Wilder was ordered to avoid combat if possible. There was no challenge to this expedition and again Rosecrans got good information about the roads he would use when his offensive pushed off.[23]

The same day Stanley took his cavalry division down the Shelbyville Pike to Fosterville and then turned southwest along the Middleton Road for yet another thrust at the Confederate cavalry post at that village. Colonel Robert Minty was leading the way when the gray pickets came in sight. He gave the order to charge and set spurs to his horse. He thought it odd that the pickets were so calmly awaiting the attack of his regiment, so he glanced over his shoulder. No one was behind him. The men had been sent down a side road by another officer. After retrieving his wayward command, Minty pitched into the 1st Alabama and 8th Confederate cavalries and ran them out of their positions. Brigadier General Will Martin, commander of the division to which these regiments belonged, reported the loss of one piece of artillery and the flag of the 1st Alabama. Stanley immediately withdrew his division but reported his rear was sniped at and harassed all the way back to their infantry lines.[24]

On May 30 Wilder was sent toward McMinnville again. There was nothing left to be destroyed, so the Confederates made no real defense; indeed, the resistance mounted by Morgan in that area had all the strength of a wet sheet of newspaper.[25] On June 3, 4, 5, 6, 10, 11, 12, and 13 small skirmishes were reported in an arc from Snow Hill in the east to Franklin in the west. While not all of these were Union offensive operations, many were. The real significance of these events is that Rosecrans so frequently penetrated the Confederate cavalry screen while Rebel probes in the vicinity of Murfreesboro did not disrupt Union activities there.

Even Confederate spies were failing to get through. In Franklin two men claiming to be Colonel Lawrence Orton and a Major Dunlop were arrested on suspicion of being spies. An investigation showed they were Confederates, Colonel W. Orton Williams and Lieutenant Walter G. Peter. Williams was a first cousin to Mrs. Robert E. Lee and was a veteran of the prewar U.S. Army. In 1862 he had killed a soldier of his Confederate command at Columbus, Kentucky, because the man did not salute him. Following that incident, Williams had no command until called upon to head one of the new regiments that Pillow was helping organize at Columbia. On his arrival, the men of the regiment refused to serve under Williams and he, apparently without telling anyone of his intentions or asking permission, donned a Union uniform and rode off to Franklin with his adjutant. There was some talk in Confederate circles that Williams was not quite right in his mind, but, be that as it may, both men were hanged on June 9.[26]

Rosecrans had established complete dominance on the eastern end of the lines and partial dominance in the area from Triune to Unionville and across to Fosterville via Middleton. Now, he could move, if he wanted to.

But did he want to? What did Bragg have planned?

Cavalry was the usual arm for intelligence gathering, but secret operations were also employed to garner information. The use of spies was made easier by the fact of divided loyalties, people behind the lines of either army whose sympathies were on the other side. Of course, this was often a Southern advantage because the war was fought on Southern soil. Wherever the Confederate armies went they would find a large part of the population friendly and anxious to share news. But the pro-Union civilians in the South gave the Yankees some help along this line, too. On April 1 Rosecrans was visited by a Dr. A. O. Habig who had just left the headquarters of Braxton Bragg and who was on his way to Washington to identify a Confederate agent working in the War Department. Bragg had helped Habig go north because Bragg thought the doctor was working for him; instead Habig was a double agent. The following month M. B. Lee gave Chief of Staff Garfield a complete and accurate description of the troop dispositions of the Army of Tennessee. Lee lived in Knoxville and had travelled via Chattanooga and Tullahoma to reach Shelbyville. From there he had crossed into Union lines. William M. R. Howell, a Unionist from eastern Tennessee, also gave Rosecrans information. "On the 13th of October I feft Loudon and travelled along the R R via Chattanooga to Wartract the road in many places was nearly impassable cars in a very worn condition & the conductor frequently ordered the passengers from one car to another. Rolling stock is very scarce on the road. Broken cars were laying nearly all along the road. As I returned on the 25th they were very busily engaged in repairing. In passing through the tunnel the cars tilted so much as to stike the sides with force enough to shatter the windows and shivver the top railing. I have lived for some time in or near the R R & say that in ordinary times no sane man would attempt to run the R R in the condition it is in & hands are not in the country to keep it up or put it in a reasonable repair. There were no fortifications around Chattanooga, saw a rifle pit dug on the 25th of October." Apparently, Howell said more than he wrote. An endorsement at the bottom of his report says "This man doubtlessly tells the truth. The plan spoken of would be attempted if support was known to be anywhere near when the attempt was made. Howell says several were hung and shot because the effort was premature. All they want to know is that we will be with them in a reasonable time."[27] It seems Rosecrans might have been dallying with the idea of having Union supporters sabotage Bragg's communications.

Not all the spies appeared as volunteers, some were employed by the Union army. These were deliberately sent south and their return was anxiously awaited. General George Thomas sent a Dr. McGowan, a Unionist from east Tennessee, to ride the railroads and report on conditions. McGowan returned the day the Tullahoma campaign opened. He had travelled in Tennessee, Georgia, and northern Alabama and found 26 engines running between Chattanooga and Tullahoma. All the engines were badly worn as were all the tracks.[28] As the campaign continued Rosecrans sent his aide-de-camp, Captain R. S. Thoms, to Chattanooga as a spy and Thoms made the trip safely. A resident of Decherd, W. B. Field, also went to Chattanooga and brought a report to Thomas who passed the information along to Rosecrans.[29]

All information was grist for the mill which slowly ground out the decision about moving the army.

As to the question of what Bragg had planned, the answer was, "Not much." On retreating from Murfreesboro, Bragg had intended to occupy the line of the Elk River, but when Rosecrans did not pursue the Army of Tennessee its commander stopped Polk's corps at Shelbyville and ordered Hardee to send troops forward to Wartrace with general army headquarters and supply dumps at Tullahoma. From their past associations in the area Generals Polk, Cheatham, and Maney all knew the country well and all understood the importance of keeping the Yankee army off the Highland Rim. If the Federals were not stopped as they came up the ridges the flat land of the rim itself made maneuver easy and defense difficult.[30] Bragg would have done well to have prepared a second position along the line of the Elk from Bethpage Bridge to Allisona Bridge. His left could have projected along the Elk toward Fayetteville while his right could have been on the Cumberland Plateau, blocking the roads from McMinnville to Chattanooga. This second line would have been reasonably compact and would have protected the rail link to Chattanooga. This means one of Bragg's mistakes was in choosing Tullahoma as a point of concentration if the line of the Duck River was forced. Tullahoma did have a road net and it was on the railroad, but it had no natural terrain advantages and could be flanked easily so as to cut the railroad.[31]

It was clear to General Johnston that the Duck River line was vulnerable for, in April, he wrote to Adjutant General Samuel Cooper that the Confederate position could be turned on its right.[32] Bragg expected to be forced back because at the time Johnston made his observation that all units of the Army of Tennessee were ordered to repair the roads in their rear and to have a staff officer from each brigade learn the roads from their position back to Tullahoma.[33]

The obvious lack of aggressive intent on Bragg's part probably contributed to the decision to weaken his army by sending reinforcements to Pemberton in Mississippi. Bragg, of course, took advantage of this decision to get rid of officers with whom he had disagreements. Thus, in May, Breckenridge was ordered to move by rail, minus his Tennessee regiments, to Atlanta and on to Mississippi. Soon McCown's men, minus their court-martialed general, would go the same route. Politics in Richmond played a part in this decision, for Mississippi had a very strong lobby in the Confederate Congress and the plight of the state was close to the president's heart.[34]

As his infantry grew fewer Bragg's strategy grew no clearer nor did his lines grow shorter. So many officers, beginning with Johnston, saw the weakness of the right flank that Bragg must have done so too. Yet the bulk of his infantry strength was placed on his left around Shelbyville and his cavalry on the crucial flank was allowed to deteriorate. It seems Bragg was quite content to give the offensive initiative to Rosecrans while having only a vague notion of how to defend against any thrust.[35]

Rosecrans developed a strategic plan slowly. He knew men and material were necessary for a forward move along with good weather, and because of the road net, the Army of the Cumberland had two options. It could operate toward the west, force Bragg out of the Cumberland Basin, and deprive the Confederates of their food-producing area. If this were accomplished Bragg might fall back or he might convince Richmond to allow him to draw on the depots at Atlanta, so that the railroad would become a true supply line, allowing him and his army to stay in middle Tennessee. If the latter became the reality Rosecrans would have accomplished very little because the Army of Tennessee would still have to be fought in order to secure middle Tennessee on a permanent basis.

These considerations made the second option appealing. By operating in the east Rosecrans could force Bragg to retreat or to fight when and where Rosecrans chose. A victory would then clear middle Tennessee with a single step instead of needing two steps. As the cavalry struggle developed Rosecrans found he could indeed do what he wanted to do. The trick would be in deciding how and when to do it.

One danger which constantly haunted Rosecrans was that of being ordered to detach troops to support another field of operations. In March, as he contemplated the large losses which had been suffered by the Army of the Potomac and the further draining away of force from that area as enlistments expired, the specter facing Rosecrans was that he would have to send men to Virginia. This reduction of the Army of the Cumberland was so real in Rosecrans' mind that he wrote to ask General H. G. Wright, commanding at Cincinnati, to write Washington arguing against any such move. Loss of men, Rosecrans argued, would force him to fall back on Nashville and to remain stationary within its defenses, allowing Van Dorn, Forrest, Morgan, et al., to run rampant over the countryside.[36]

With the passing of time the pendulum swung in the opposite direction. After Chancellorsville it looked as if a quick and decisive Union victory was needed to prop up the administration. The expectation became that General Grant would be ordered to give up his seemingly futile drive on Vicksburg to reinforce both the Army of the Cumberland and Burnside's force in Kentucky, so these two could then march on Chattanooga and Knoxville. In this case the goal would be only partly military, for such an advance would bring within friendly lines the Unionist population of east Tennessee, thus achieving a political goal.[37]

When this scenario did not occur, and when Grant did get his claws set in Vicksburg's defenses, calls for manpower began to come from quite another direction. After early June more and more of the Union forces in west Tennessee and Kentucky were being sent to help Grant. From Memphis General Samuel A. Hurlbut reported he had abandoned Jackson, Tennessee, because he did not have the forces to hold it. This left a huge hole which cried out for a Confederate cavalry raid to sweep through, a raid which could very well penetrate deep into Kentucky. Both Hurlbut and General Alexander S. Asboth at Columbus, Kentucky, wanted Rosecrans to send men to replace those they had sent Grant.[38] Rosecrans could move or he could watch his force dribble away as reinforcements to Grant's secondary line.

On June 8 the commanding general sent a circular to all corps and division commanders in the Army of the Cumberland asking their written opinions as to whether or not Bragg had been seriously weakened by sending reinforcements to Mississippi, what were their estimates for a victory against Bragg, and whether a quick advance was called for.[39] The answers came back rather quickly. No one urged an immediate advance, the general opinion was to wait and see what happened at Vicksburg. As chief of staff, James A. Garfield had the task of summarizing the answers to the circular but as a staff officer he, technically, had no voice in such a council of war. Garfield ignored the tradition that staff officers did not participate in such matters and gave Rosecrans his opinion. His was a clear call for action, "The Government and the War Department believe this Army ought to move against the enemy."[40]

Rosecrans listened to his chief of staff. Swiftly his strategy came together. The Army of the Cumberland would make a massive feint towards Bragg's left while striking with its own left toward Manchester, and beyond, at the road and rail bridges over the Elk River.

Chapter Three
The Struggle

Before daylight on June 23 the blue cavalry columns responded to the bugle call and moved out from their bivouacs. The destination of this force, commanded by General Stanley and supervised by Major General Gordon Granger, was familiar territory. Once more, there would be a push against the Confederates around Unionville and the outposts at Rover and Middleton. Only this was to be different, this time the blue riders would not be returning to their old camps, this advance was the beginning of the real thing. It was rather cool for late June in Tennessee and dry—the last dry day for the next 11 days. The Tullahoma campaign would be fought in an almost constant rain, a condition which would have serious consequences for Rosecrans and would produce the only good results Bragg would achieve. From January 5 to June 23, the Army of the Cumberland had been halted 169 days.[1] Rosecrans' actions would have to vindicate his decisions.

Stanley and the bulk of the cavalry were at Triune and advanced down the Lewisburg Pike until they reached the left-hand fork which led towards Shelbyville. With the 9th Pennsylvania Cavalry in the lead, the Yankee force soon reached Eagleville, a town they had visited before. Just beyond the village Confederate resistance was encountered and a slow, running fight developed with the 2nd and 4th Georgia and the 7th and 51st Alabama Cavalry who were supported by a battery. The Confederate pickets fell back from hill to hill, always pausing long enough to force the Union cavalry to dismount, deploy, and advance. The country was broken and much of it was covered in cedar thickets, so the advance took a good deal of work and used up a great deal of energy. After two miles of stop-and-go work the 2nd Michigan Cavalry relieved the Pennsylvania boys.[2]

The fight eventually reached the village of Rover and the Michiganders took the abandoned camp of the Reb picket post there, some "shebangs" consisting of rubber ponchos stretched over fence rails and a few cooking utensils. Encouraged by this small success, the Federal force pushed on until they came near Unionville, the first infantry outpost of the main line held by Polk's infantry. Using a road not shown on the Union maps, Southern infantry mounted a flank attack and there was some sharp fighting until the 4th Kentucky and 1st East Tennessee (U.S.) stabilized the situation. During this skirmish there occurred an event which must have been as terrifying to the participant as it is amazing to a reader. Captain Marshall Thatcher of the Union cavalry said that just after the flank attack had been repulsed "a single horseman was seen to leave the enemy's ranks and charge down alone upon our brigade in front of the First Tennessee. Nearly every man in that regiment and not a few from the Second fired at the charging figure, and at last they stopped in blank amazement that the man was able to sit bolt upright in face of that shower of bullets. But he still came thundering on, while hostilities ceased on both sides to look and wonder if the man was made of iron, or had a charmed life. He soon rode in among the Federal troops and the mystery was explained. A bullet had cut both reins, and the horse refused to cease charging; all that the rider could do was grasp the horse's mane and pommel of the saddle and hang on. His clothes were riddled and the horse had many a scratch, but the man's skin was whole, though it may be doubted if he breathed during his ride." Night put an end to the fighting[3] but Rosecrans had accomplished his goal of diverting Bragg's attention to the western area even though no great gains had been made.

Back in Murfreesboro, clerks were busy at headquarters making copies of orders and soon couriers were galloping to the various camps to deliver the envelopes containing Rosecrans' instructions and then returning with an officer's signature on the envelope to acknowledge receipt. It was the intention of the commanding general that the army should travel light. The infantry was to march from Murfreesboro with rations for 12 days. The men would carry three days' rations of hard bread, coffee, sugar, and salt in haversacks with the rest accompanying each regiment in wagons, six or seven being the maximum number of wagons allowed. Two boxes of the appropriate caliber cartridges were to be carried for each company in addition to those in each soldier's cartridge box. Beef for six days would be driven along on the hoof. Each regiment could have one ambulance with each brigade maintaining a reserve train of 10 ambulances.[4]

When the issue became one of personal baggage the same emphasis was placed on travelling light. General officers could have 125 pounds of baggage, field officers could take 100, and line officers could move 80 pounds of personal belongings. Enlisted men were allowed one blanket, two pairs of drawers, two pairs of socks, one jacket, one pair pants, one pair shoes, and one hat. Since most of this would be worn that left one pair of drawers and one pair of socks to go in knapsacks along with the blanket.[5] Nothing else would be allowed, too much depended on rapid movement.

Utilizing the road net, Major General Thomas L. Crittenden was to move his corps east through Bradyville and, at Lumley's Stand, turn south through the community of Pocahontas to attack Manchester from the north. This would lead Crittenden wide around Bragg's right and would bring him back into the strategic picture behind the Confederate flank and nearer to the N&C Railroad bridge over Elk River than any Rebel infantry. Rosecrans was so convinced of the deterioration of the Confederate cavalry in the Bradyville area he sent only one division of cavalry, Turchin's, to accompany this move and then detached one brigade, Minty's, before the expedition left, leaving only one brigade of horsemen under Colonel Eli Long to accompany what he considered to be his main striking force. Thomas was to support Crittenden by moving out along the Manchester Pike and attracting all the attention he could at Hoover's Gap. Once Crittenden was behind the Confederate flank Thomas would shift to his left and move up to join Crittenden. Meanwhile, McCook was to move along the Liberty Pike and attack Liberty Gap. This was to be a diversion in favor of Crittenden's main move, however, and as soon as Thomas left Hoover's Gap to move forward McCook was to abandon the Liberty Gap attack and shift left to follow Thomas. To complete the move, Major General Gordon Granger would lead the Reserve Corps down the Shelbyville Pike to attract additional attention toward the area already made sensitive by Stanley's all-day cavalry skirmish around Unionville. Granger was to resort to the well-used but still effective ruse of building lots of campfires to make his force seem larger than it was.[6]

Early on the morning of Thursday, June 24, the Union infantry began to march, but not the cavalry on the western end of the line. During the night Stanley had pulled back to the Rover area and his men arose to a wet and hungry bivouac. The rain, which would continue throughout the campaign, had set in during the night. Also, planning had gone awry and no one had thought to send food for the horses and none was to be had in the vicinity, for the area had been thoroughly foraged by both sides. Moreover, the men had only the rations they carried on their persons.[7]

About noon, Brigadier Robert Mitchell, commanding the 1st Cavalry Division, was ordered to attack Middleton and then to await support there. Accordingly, Mitchell pulled back to Eagleville and turned east to attack the village. About a mile west of Middleton, Confederate pickets opened fire on the blue column, but the main Southern line was on high ground beyond the town. Reaching this line proved to be something of a problem. Several of the structures in the village were sturdy log buildings, as opposed to clapboard, and these had been taken over by some very determined Rebel sharpshooters. One battalion of the 9th Pennsylvania advanced on foot but was paying a high price for their gains. Calling them back, Mitchell opened fire on the sharpshooter nests with his artillery and, soon shell fire had shingle roofs ablaze. As the Johnnies fell back the 2nd Michigan moved in to occupy the village. There were elements of three Confederate cavalry units at Middleton[8] and, being badly outnumbered, they fell back but kept the Union force under observation. Soon Minty's Brigade of Turchin's Division rode up to reinforce Mitchell's Division, not that Mitchell needed help, and the combined force traveled east and north to Christiana on the main pike from Murfreesboro to Shelbyville.[9] These units would not move again until Sunday, June 27.

The infantry probably envied the cavalry, their noonday start. They had gotten up in the dark and, by daybreak were marching down roads increasingly deep in mud. Crittenden's 21st Army Corps was to make the main advance, so his men, led by John Palmer's Division, moved from their bivouacs at Cripple Creek and Readyville along the road toward Bradyville. The key position to be reached that day was Gilley's Hill which, Palmer had been told, had been guarded only by a cavalry patrol as recently as June 5. It still was. Palmer fought a brief skirmish, losing one man killed and one wounded,[10] but in the vicinity of the gap the entire army corps stopped. The problem was not Rebel opposition but Tennessee mud. General Thomas J. Wood, commanding Crittenden's 1st Division, said, "It has scarcely ever been my misfortune in eighteen years of active service (during which I have marched many thousands of miles) to have to pass over so bad a road. The geological formation of the plateau . . . is such as to make in wet weather the very worst roads conveyable. The soil is a mixture of clay and sand, which under the continual fall of rain became with the slightest travel a almost impassable quagmire."[11] Crittenden had with him four companies of Pioneers, provided by Brigadier J. St. Clair Morton of the Pioneer Brigade, but even with their road improvements he found it necessary to assign 50 men to each wagon to help the teams up hills. In five days, June 24–28, Crittenden would manage to cover only 21 miles.[12] The main thrust planned by Rosecrans had bogged down in the most literal sense. Fortunately, "Old Rosy" was flexible enough to improvise as the day's events unfolded.

Major General McCook led off his XX Army Corps by sending Colonel Luther Bradley's 3rd Brigade, 3rd Division, down the Shelbyville Pike to the village of Christiana. Bradley was to occupy the crossroads and allow the rest of the corps to pass along the Liberty Pike towards Liberty Gap. Approximately three miles south of Murfreesboro, atop a sharp little hill known as "The Knob," Confederates opened fire. From there until he reached Christiana, Bradley's Yankees had to contend with gray cavalry and some light horse artillery[13] but this force could not stop an infantry brigade which was backed up by the rest of Phil Sheridan's Division.

The rest of McCook's Corps, led by R. W. Johnson's Division, passed through Christiana and on towards Liberty Gap. Waiting for them were the men of Patrick Cleburne's Division, some of the most tenacious fighters in the Army of Tennessee, commanded by its best combat leader.

Liberty Gap is only one of a series of breaks in the hills at the spot where Liberty Pike climbs the ridge to the village of Bell Buckle. To the east of Liberty Gap, about one-half mile distant, is another gap passable for infantry and cavalry. Near the Fugett house at the foot of Bald Knob was another pass which could be used by artillery as well as horse and foot. The railroad ran through yet another gap just to the west and the hills could be climbed by infantry at any given point.[14]

Cleburne's brigadier on the ground was St. John Liddell, an experienced commander who had proven dependable on many fields. From January 9 to April 24 Liddell's Brigade was in winter quarters at Wartrace. The general and his men were ordered to Bell Buckle on April 24 but not until June 6 was he ordered to picket Liberty Gap with two regiments and two guns. Liddell was also told to send a small force to guard the railroad gap.[15] Actually in command in the gap itself was Colonel Lucius Featherston who had at his disposal 540 infantry in his own 5th Arkansas and Colonel J. E. Josey's consolidated 13th/15th Arkansas. Featherston positioned his 5th Arkansas to the left of the gap as one faced outward, while Josey's 13th/15th Consolidated Arkansas held the right. Colonel Snyder had the 6th/7th Consolidated Arkansas in nearby support and Colonel Govan had his 2nd Arkansas in Bell Buckle. The command post for this force was Liberty Church.[16]

Liddell's Brigade had held a drill for their corps commander, General Hardee, on June 1 and a visiting Englishman, Colonel Arthur Freemantle, witnessed the event which he later described. "General Liddell's Brigade was composed of Arkansas troops—five very weak regiments which had suffered severely in the different battles . . . The men were good-sized, healthy, and well clothed, but without

Major General Patrick Cleburne

This photo was made in 1864, only weeks before the general was killed at Franklin, Tennessee.

any attempt at uniformity in color or cut; but nearly all were dressed in either gray or brown coats and felt hats . . . Most of them were armed with Enfield rifles captured from the enemy. Each regiment carried a 'battle flag', blue, with a white border . . . They drilled tolerably well, and an advance in line was remarkably good."[17]

One and a half miles in advance of the Confederate position was a cavalry advance guard. On the eastern side of the Liberty Pike the consolidated 1st/3rd Kentucky Cavalry were placed as pickets while Martin's cavalry was on the west. Coming into position against them were five companies of the 39th Indiana Mounted Infantry led by Colonel T. J. Harrison with General August Willich leading his 1st Brigade of Johnson's Division close behind. This advance captured three Johnnie Rebs who were cutting wheat near the road.[18] Bragg's supply problem obviously had grown intense. Not only were soldiers cutting wheat, they were cutting it while it was wet. That grain would have to be consumed quickly else it would rot.

About noon, as Colonel Featherston was sitting down to dinner, a courier arrived with news that Yankee cavalry had attacked the Confederate pickets at Old Millersburg. The colonel sent the courier on to Bell Buckle to inform General Liddell of this development, but the first rider was not out of sight before a second arrived to say the enemy was going into line in front of Liberty Gap. A deployment plan had already been agreed to between Featherston and Josey and, leaving Josey to put that into force, the commander rode out to scout the approaching blue force. Featherston had gone less than 300 yards before he was fired on.[19] Colonel Josey had 365 men in his 13th/15th Arkansas, so he sent three companies across the gap to help the 5th Arkansas, which could muster only 175 rifles. Then, he had to send two companies to guard the pass to his east while another company was already posted one and a half miles away at yet another pass.[20] This means the total Confederate force in the gap was about 540 before Josey sent two companies to the east. This detachment would probably have been 75 to 80 men, leaving 465 or so Rebs to oppose the three brigades of Johnson's Division.

As the troops in blue approached Liberty Gap, Colonel Philemon P. Baldwin, commander of the 3rd Brigade, described what he saw. "The enemy's position was on a chain of hills 400 yards from where we deployed. The road, on reaching the base of the hills, turned square to the left, and followed along their base for 500 yards, to where the hills extended across the road. Their main force was posted where the road enters the hills."[21]

As General Willich led his men into position he was actually happy to be on a battlefield. Willich had been captured at Murfreesboro and had been exchanged only a few days earlier. As his men came up Willich placed the 15th Ohio under Lt. Col. Frank Askins to the right of the road and the 49th Ohio, led by Colonel William Gibson, to the left. In support of the 15th Ohio was Colonel Harrison's 39th Indiana Mounted Infantry, now on foot, while the 32nd Indiana under Major Glass supported the 49th Ohio. The 89th Illinois under Colonel C. T. Hotchkiss was held in reserve.[22] Since Willich was preparing to attack directly into the gap he would face fire from the Confederates on either side of the pass but his attack would eventually slant off to his right to confront the Southern left under Featherston.

Askins' 15th Ohio moved out first. The Confederate position he faced was to the right as he faced toward the gap and atop a steep hill which was cleared at the bottom but which was covered with timber towards the top with a fence along the woods line.[23] Across the Liberty Pike Colonel Gibson deployed the 49th Ohio to confront Josey's Confederates, with the 32nd Indiana protecting his left flank. The two Union units had to cross about 150 yards of open ground and attack up the hills which marked the sides of the gap.[24]

As the Yanks on both sides of the road moved forward they met a "furious" fire and the attackers found themselves in the uncomfortable position of being in the open while being shot at by an opponent hidden in the tree line. Willich decided taking the gap frontally was going to cost a great many lives, especially when the flanks of the position were open, so he called for help from Colonel Baldwin and his 3rd Brigade. About 4:00 p.m. the Louisville Legion of Infantry under Colonel William Berry moved on the right of the road to help out the 15th Ohio and 39th Indiana while the 6th Indiana went to the left to reinforce the 49th Ohio and 32nd Indiana. To add additional weight to the attack Baldwin sent Lt. Col. David Dunn with the 29th Indiana and Colonel Thomas Rose of the 77th Pennsylvania to extend the Union right and overlap the Confederate left.[25] By this time the attackers were getting close to the foot of the hill and were benefiting from a common error made by defenders of high ground. In shooting down hill there is a tendency to fire too high and this was happening. The flank attack mounted by the 29th Indiana and 77th Pennsylvania struck undefended ground but, even so, moved slowly. Colonel Rose noted that they attacked over ground so steep "we were obliged to scramble up by laying hold of bushes and saplings to effect progress.[26]

Cleburne had come forward to oversee his Arkansas boys in the fight. He saw Josey's's men give way first but, even so, Featherston held on for the better part of another hour, checking the frontal attack and falling back before the threat to his flank. By the time the Yankee flankers were in a position to cause danger it was raining hard and almost dark, so Cleburne ordered a withdrawal across Wartrace Creek to the next line of hills where the rest of Liddell's men were already waiting. Liddell recalled: "After contending the ground as long as tenable with my small force, I withdrew to the next range of knobs, one mile further back, out in full view and hurried forward the rest of my brigade."[27] Among those left in the gap was the body of Captain L. R. Frisk of the 5th Arkansas, a recent immigrant from Sweden.[28] Cleburne was not worried about the next day. From Liberty Gap almost all the way to Bell Buckle the country was a succession of steep ridges and narrow valleys, a terrain ready-made for defensive delaying tactics.

Had there been quiet at Liberty Gap the men there could have heard the sounds of fighting at the eastern mouth of Hoover's Gap where Colonel John Wilder was engaged in the process of creating a legend—the legend of the Spencer repeater.

Wilder's mounted infantry, officially the 1st Brigade of Joseph Reynold's 4th Division of George Thomas' XIV Army Corps, had moved out of its camp seven miles north of Murfreesboro at 3:00 a.m. They had covered 14 miles when contact was made with Confederate cavalry at Big Spring Branch. The 72nd Indiana under Colonel Miller was leading the way for Wilder, preceded by an advance guard of five companies of the 72nd commanded by Lieutenant Colonel Kilpatrick, which, in turn, was preceded by a vidette of 25 men. The first shots were fired about a mile beyond Big Spring Branch. The Southern cavalry had taken up position on one of the ubiquitous cedar-covered knobs but the rapidly advancing five companies pushed them back and Kilpatrick seized the light fortifications at the mouth of Hoover's Gap before they could be manned. The only Rebel forces present were a squadron of the 1st/3rd Consolidated Kentucky and they scattered before the Union charge, losing their battle flag.[29] The other squadron of that regiment also had an equally bad morning at Liberty Gap. Of course, the fact that only a squadron was picketing each of two very important roads illustrates the collapsing strength and capacity of the Confederate cavalry under Wheeler.

Stretching in front of Wilder's men was the four-mile length of Hoover's Gap, flanked by ridges which rise 200 to 300 feet above the floor of the gap, and in places so narrow two wagons could not pass each other. From the nominally eastern end of the gap it was only 11 miles on a direct road to Manchester, by way of the village of Beech Grove, and the rear of Bragg's right flank. Prisoners who Wilder knew said that more cavalry was on the Garrison Fork about

Colonel John Wilder

This photograph shows him in the years after the war. Wilder became mayor of Chattanooga, Tennessee.

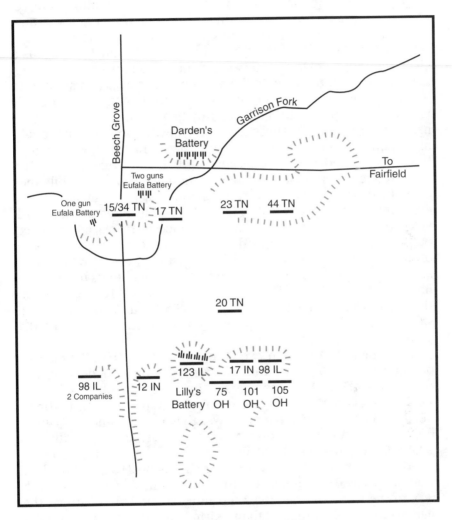

Beech Grove

Garrison Fork

Darden's Battery

Two guns Eufala Battery

One gun Eufala Battery

15/34 TN — 17 TN

23 TN 44 TN

To Fairfield

20 TN

123 IL

17 IN 98 IL

98 IL
2 Companies

12 IN

Lilly's Battery

75 OH

101 OH

105 OH

Hoover's Gap, June 24, 1863

Map drawn by author

two miles past the mouth of the gap, and that a Confederate infantry unit was near Fairfield, some five miles south of Beech Grove. Although he was already six miles ahead of the infantry Wilder decided to push on to the exit from the gap and hold it until reinforcements could catch up.[30] Not sparing the horses, Wilder quickly came to the mouth of the gap and sent his brigade into position.

Just to the right of the gap as one faced nominally east was a steep hill topped by a cemetery which dated to pioneer times. Colonel Miller placed the 72nd Indiana among the graves and supported his disposition by deploying two mountain howitzers from Lilly's Battery on the point of the hill slightly behind the crest where they had some protection.[31] These mountain howitzers were well thought of by some people, not so by others. At any rate, Lilly had four of the twelve pounders which, because of their short tubes, had only a short range but were of light construction and were so mobile they could be disassembled and carried on mule back. These pieces were excellent for spewing canister. Lilly also commanded six standard-sized pieces, ten-pounder Rodmans, which were placed on a secondary hill facing south toward Fairfield. The Rodman was the basic ordnance rifle made of wrought iron. The tube weighed 820 pounds and it fired a projectile weighing just under ten pounds using a one-pound powder charge. The range allowed by the 12 degree elevation permitted by the gun carriage was 3,500 yards, but if the trail was dropped into a hole the range could be lengthened to 6,000 yards.[32]

To the left of the gap two companies of the 98th Illinois took position while 400 yards wide to the right, on a high ridge, four companies of the 17th Indiana set up a defensive line. When the 123rd Illlinois came up they were placed in support of the Rodmans of Lilly's Battery. The 17th Indiana was the most seasoned of Wilder's units having fought at Corinth, Munfordville, and Perryville. The 123rd Illinois has fought at Perryville, despite having been mustered into service only a few days earlier, losing 216 men killed and wounded. The 98th Illinois had lost 83 men in a train wreck on the way to the front, but like the 72nd Indiana and Lilly's Battery, they had seen no combat other than skirmishing during the preceding winter.[33]

Most of this development came as a complete surprise to the Confederate infantry commander at Fairfield, General William Bate. Bate, a strong supporter of Bragg, was part of the newly formed division of A. P. Stewart. His brigade included the 20th Tennessee under Colonel Thomas R. Smith, the 9th Alabama Battalion, the 37th Georgia, a Tennessee unit which had been created only a week before called the 15th/37th Consolidated under Colonel R. C. Tyler,

Caswell's Georgia Battalion of Sharpshooters, and two batteries of artillery, the Eufala Battery and Maney's Battery. This would be the last battle for Maney's Battery since it was in the process of being broken up and the men reassigned to the 24th Sharpshooter Battalion. Since Bragg did not have enough infantry to defend all the gaps in the area he had ordered Hardee to concentrate a force at Fairfield, a central position from which troops could be shifted to any threatened point. Bate had already started moving forward when, about two o'clock, he received orders from Corps Commander Hardee to march toward the gap. En route he met Colonel J. R. Butler of the 1st/3rd Kentucky Cavalry who told Bate his command had been scattered by the Union advance.[34] To protect his advance, Bate sent forward Major Fred Claybrook and several companies of the 20th Tennessee to act as skirmishers. As Claybrook came in contact with skirmishers thrown out by Wilder the Confederates under Bate began to form line. The 650 men in the brigade were positioned at right angles to the Fairfield Road with their left flank on the east bank of the Garrison Fork. The skirmishers potshotted each other for about a mile as the Yanks slowly fell back to their main line.[35]

Seeing Bate approach, Wilder shifted men to his right. The remainder of the 17th Indiana and the 98th Illinois were sent to reinforce the four companies of the 17th already on the right. These men would be needed.[36] As Bate reached the immediate vicinity of the mouth of the gap he shifted his men west of Garrison Fork to secure the hills in that area and opened fire with his artillery. Initially, these guns did effective work, killing all the mules and two of the gunners at one of the Yankee mountain howitzers. Lilly quickly replied with his Rodmans, dismounting one of Bate's pieces and forcing the two batteries to shift position. Bate, however, crowded forward his infantry, pressing his attack so hotly that Wilder started three more regiments toward his right, the 75th, 101st, and the 105th Ohio. Bate apparently did not see Lilly's guns because in making his attack he allowed his line to present a flank to the hill where Lilly was posted, supported by the 123rd Illinois. It is quite possible that the heavily falling rain, combined with gun smoke, obscured the artillery position. As the 20th Tennessee swept forward it caught fire from front and flank, nevertheless, the attack they led got to within less that 20 yards of the Yankee line. But before the reinforcing regiments could arrive the fire from the Spencers of the 17th Indiana and the 98th Illinois had stopped the Confederate assault. The Spencer was a .52 caliber using a seven shot tube magazine which was mounted in the gun stock. Additional tubes could be loaded and carried into battle, so an almost continuous blaze of fire could be kept up.[37] The Spencer became known as "the gun the Yankees load on Sunday and shoot all week."

Bate pulled back slightly, secured his flanks, and waited for help. Of the 650 men he had taken into battle 150 had become casualties. From the Union side of the line the attack looked like a slaughter. "The poor regiment was literally cut to pieces, and but few men of the 20th Tennessee that attempted the charge would ever charge again."[38] From the Confederate side it was merely a repulse. "The 20th Tennessee was outflanked. That unit found a stone fence perpendicular to the line of battle and reformed to protect the flank. Our artillery was repositioned on a high hill near the William Johnson house, and the situation stabilized."[39] The 20th Tennessee would be cut to pieces, but not until December 1864 at the Battle of Nashville while holding the hill which still bears the name of its commander on that occasion, Colonel William Shy.

Reinforcements were approaching Hoover's Gap from different directions and it was a question as to who would arrive first. Indeed, at one point Wilder had received orders from General Thomas to pull back. Wilder refused to obey the order and told the staff officer delivering it that he would bear full responsibility for his act. Later, Thomas thanked Wilder for what he had done.

From the direction of Fairfield came Bushrod Johnson's Confederate Brigade. Johnson started for Hoover's Gap sometime after 4:00 p.m. after hearing that Union troops had penetrated the gap. His four regiments were the 44th Tennessee under Colonel John Fulton, the 17th commanded by Colonel Albert Marks, the 23rd led by Colonel R. H. Keeble, containing men who were recruited in the immediate vicinity of Beech Grove by the original commander of the unit, Colonel Mathias (Matt) Martin, and some remains of the 37th Tennessee which had refused to be consolidated with the 15th and assigned to Bate's Brigade.[40] Thirteen officers of the 37th had resigned over the issue of consolidation but their resignations had been refused. Apparently the dissension which wracked the high command of the Army of Tennessee was also present at the lower ranks. This brigade was also an example of the problems with armament that Bragg had been unable to solve during the winter. In the 44th Tennessee only one company had rifles, the rest had smoothbore muskets. These men reached the gap about 6:00 p.m. When arriving on the field Johnson quickly consulted with Bate and decided to hit the Union center with its cluster of Rodman cannon. This attack was made with two regiments, but as they advanced, three companies of the 123rd Ohio sprang into view from a ravine they were occupying in advance of Lilly's guns, the 72nd Indiana opened an oblique enfilade from the cemetery with their repeaters and the Rodman blasted canister. The Tennesseeans of Johnson's Brigade had done some good fighting in the past and would do

Major General A. P. Stewart

The new division commander was fighting in his own door-yard. His home was in Winchester, Tennessee.

Major General George H. Thomas

Chickamauga-Chattanooga National Battlefield Park

more in the future, but this fire was too much. The gray infantry fell back. As the attack was ending Brigadier George Crook arrived on the field and sent up the 92nd Ohio and the 18th Kentucky to relieve the center of Wilder's line.

At sundown Johnson placed one section of Darden's Battery on the south side of the Manchester Pike to link up with Bate's right flank. The 23rd Tennessee was on the east bank of Garrison Fork while the 20th Tennessee occupied a hill west of that stream. The 17th Tennessee was on a conical hill 1,200 yards west of the creek and some 600 yards beyond the 20th Tennessee. During the night the 44th Tennessee, which had been guarding another road, came up and replaced the 23rd which then moved west of Garrison Fork.[41]

The first day of the Tullahoma campaign came to an end in darkness and rain. Wilder had lost 14 killed, including J. R. Eddy, chaplain of the 72nd Indiana, and 47 wounded, one of whom, James Bigham, died during the night. He had been shot through the knee by a Reb sharpshooter and his leg had been amputated. Lilly's Battery had fired 350 rounds and repeating rifles had been used on a large scale for the first time in warfare. Henry Campbell of Lilly's Battery did not care. "I found an empty hog trough and slept in that to keep out of the mud." The Cincinnati *Gazette*, a few days later, said, "Thus, the first and most critical step of the campaign was won by Wilder's soldiership."

From the Confederate side came a poignant note. William Bate said in his report, "Lieutenant Aaron Bate, a young man of 17 years of age, and my volunteer aide, did well his part. I regret his death, which resulted from the exposure and exhaustion of that day."[42] Across a blank page in a notebook belonging to his dead young kinsman the general wrote, "This remarkable young man, the most intellectual of our family, died the death of a patriot, soldier, and Christian philosopher.[43]

June 25 was a wet day but it was surprisingly quiet over much of the far-flung field of maneuver. On the Union right, Lieutenant Colonel Patrick took the 5th Iowa and 4th Michigan Cavalry down the Shelbyville Pike to see what was going on between Fosterville and Guys Gap. What he found was Wharton's cavalry division supported by a brigade of Polk's infantry and a battery.[44] This was more action than Patrick wanted, so he fell back to Christiana.

On the far Union left most of the effort went into trying to move the ammunition and supply wagons up Gilley's Gap. This was a very slow and laborious process, but while it was going on Colonel Eli Long led his cavalry brigade out on a scout. At Lumley's Stand the colonel reported capturing "three suspicious appearing persons, one of whom proved to be a notorious character." At Noah's Fork and at Pocahontas a Confederate courier station was discovered and one man was captured at each place.[45] This scout is more significant than these results make it sound to have been. Lumley's Stand was the crossing of the McMinnville-Shelbyville road with the Bradyville-Manchester road. The total absence of Confederate cavalry shows Bragg's flank was wide open and that he knew nothing of one of the major threats to his army.

Most of the noise and excitement of June 25 would be at Liberty Gap. Cleburne had already brought up S. A. M. Wood's Brigade to reinforce Liddell, but there was not enough room to deploy both units, so Liddell stayed in advance with Wood in hand in case of need. The 8th Arkansas was placed by Colonel Kelly in the Railroad Gap; Govan and the 2nd Arkansas were placed south of Wartrace Creek; Featherston and Josey placed their commands on knobs while Lt. Col. Peter Snyder took the 6th/7th Arkansas about one-half mile west of the Sugg's farm along a line of hills.[46]

General August Willich was the man in charge in the gap for the Union. He posted his line beginning with the 32nd Indiana on the left and crossing the Bell Buckle Road to link with the 89th Illinois which would constitute his right wing. The 15th Ohio supported his left and the 49th Ohio supported his right. Although the entire force of McCook's Corps was available, orders had gone out not to press an attack unless there was a Confederate collapse. Liberty Gap was to be a feint supporting what had become the main thrust at Hoover's Gap.[47]

Between the two forces in Liberty Gap was an open field which varied from 500 to 2,000 yards across. To the west of the Bell Buckle Road, as Liberty Pike was called after passing the gap, was a slight hill in the middle of the open field. To the east Wartrace Creek flowed along the foot of the hills occupied by the Confederates, creating a bluff a few feet in height and adding to the strength of that position.[48]

Colonel Featherston reported that his 5th Arkansas deployed some 75 men as skirmishers in the field in front of his line with the rest of his regiment, only about 100 men, remaining quietly on their knob. Along with Josey's men from the 13th/15th they made several forays into the corn field to keep the Yankee skirmishers at a respectful distance and in this bickering of small forces the hill in the corn field changed hands several times. From the Northern side things looked a little different. Colonel Charles Hotchkiss of the 89th Illinois reported that "about 10:00 skirmishers appeared. About noon a strong attack was made along the road and against the junction with the 32nd Indiana. Three attacks were made between noon and 3:00 p.m. with each being repulsed." According to Southern reports, each of the "attacks" was made by between 30 and 50 skirmishers advancing and then fading back, in and out of the corn.[49]

Around 3:00 p.m. things became more serious. The front Union line, composed of the 32nd Indiana, 89th Illinois, and 30th Indiana, was beginning to run out of ammunition. The 15th Ohio moved up from its support position and shared its cartridges while the dead and wounded were relieved of theirs. This activity was necessary because a Rebel battleline of significant force was rolling across the corn field, preceded by a cloud of skirmishers. This attack was intended to give the Union line a push to determine how strong it was. When the Yanks showed an inclination to stay put, the Johnnies went to ground where the terrain offered cover. A Union soldier described the next events. "From eighty to 320 feet in front of our position was a low rail fence. A cornfield stretched 400 yards to a hill in the field, and about 100 yards from the fence was a small gulley. The Confederate forces were now in the gulley and around an orchard and buildings on our right. The 49th Ohio came forward out of reserve and drove the enemy out of his position by the tactic of 'advance, firing.'"[50] The "advance, firing" tactic was executed by forming the regiment in four ranks. As the front rank fired the successive ranks passed through their line, advanced a set distance, halted, and the next front rank fired. By the time the fourth rank had rotated to the front and fired the original front rank had reloaded and was ready to take the advance.

During this attack Willich had called up reinforcements. The 77th Pennsylvania under Colonel Miller moved up into a supporting position on the Union left with the 79th Illinois, led by Colonel Allen Buckner, extending their line to the east. Behind these units came the 38th Illinois, the 38th Ohio, and the 101st Ohio. There were now a large number of fresh Federal troops in line in Liberty Gap. One of them, however, had just become a victim of a new weapon which had reached the Confederates during the winter. Colonel Miller of the 77th Pennsylvania was killed by a sharpshooter firing at a range of almost one thousand yards.[51]

During the winter some British made Whitworth rifles equipped with telescopic sights had made it through the naval blockade and, in due time, a few of these rifles had reached the Army of Tennessee. The share which fell to Cleburne's Division was five. A series of shooting matches were held to pick the best shots and, once chosen, Cleburne put the men through some rigid training. He placed these men in a line at distances varying from 500 to 1,000 yards apart and had them estimate the distance to the next man. Having made the estimate, they paced off the distance to check their accuracy. By the time of the Liberty Gap engagement these men had

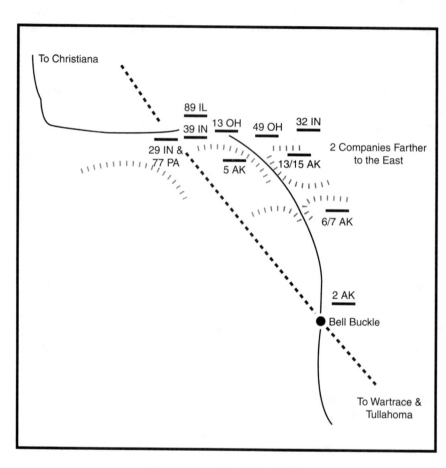

Liberty Gap, June 24, 1863

Map drawn by author

become quite adept at estimating distances. They were already adept at hitting their targets.[52]

At about four o'clock Cleburne received a report from the cavalry commander in the area, Lt. Col. Paul Anderson, that the Yanks were falling back from the area of New Fosterville. This was true, in part. The men of McCook's Corps not engaged at Liberty Gap were beginning to shift toward the east where they would follow Thomas at Hoover's Gap, in keeping with the established Union plan. Cleburne, however, knew nothing of the Union plans and motives. A retreat was a retreat and should be speeded up, if possible, so a shove was in order to see if the Yanks would fall back. Once more Featherston sent his skirmishers across the corn field with Josey joining him. The boys in blue on their front showed some signs of wavering, so Govan led the 2nd Arkansas forward. The wavering in the Union lines came when the reinforcements sent forward earlier moved into the front line to replace regiments which had fired away all or most of their cartridges and the confusion was more apparent than real. Finding the Union line solid, the Rebs fell back to their original position.[53]

This time the Federal command decided to push some themselves. Colonel Rose, now commanding the 77th Pennsylvania, saw in front of him "a corn field 400 to 500 yards wide bounded by a range of hills 60–100 feet high. The main Confederate force was on these hills with their artillery on their left."[54] Joining Rose's line would be the 79th, 34th, and 38th Illinois. All four regiments would crash into Govan's 2nd Arkansas.

The advance across the corn field was slow because of the mud. Given the amount of rain which had fallen the infantrymen must have had clods of soil the size of dinner plates adhering to each shoe making a nightmare parody of any attempt to charge, especially when this slow-motion movement was coupled with the "zip" of Whitworth bullets and the sound of these impacting human flesh. Colonel Brickner, 79th Illinois, said "the effect of their sharpshooters was terrible." Colonel Rose remembered "the plain we were obliged to cross was of mud, shoe-top deep."[53] Three times the Union troops surged across the field with a different regiment leading the way, and three times blasts of rifle fire from the 2nd Arkansas drove them back. Govan had taken position behind a fence just a few feet from the base of the hill but now his ammunition was running low. A few men tried to carry reserve supplies down from the crest of the ridge but there was a good deal of Union fire sweeping their path. A fourth time the blue line came on, led now by the 38th Illinois. As the fire from his line began to sputter out as men emptied their cartridge boxes Govan gave the order to pull back to the ridge crest where ammunition was waiting. Liddell supported this

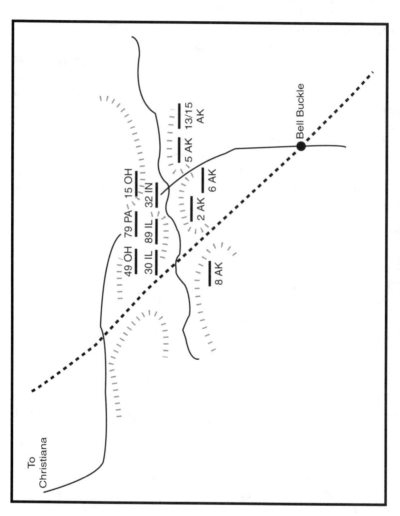

To Christiana

49 OH 79 PA 15 OH
30 IL 89 IL 32 IN

8 AK

2 AK

6 AK

5 AK 13/15 AK

Bell Buckle

Liberty Gap, June 25, 1863

Map drawn by author

move, "Colonel Govan urged me not to fight any longer to maintain a position which was of no avail in the general result. I told him, 'No, hold on. I must obey the orders, whatever my own views or opinions are, and I will stay there until ordered or forced away.'" As the Johnnies slowly went up the hill, turning to fire off their last rounds, the color bearer of the 2nd Arkansas went down and slid down a steep place, almost to the advancing Union line. The battle flag of the 2nd Arkansas literally fell into the hands of the Yankees.[56]

By now darkness was falling, along with more rain, and the two forces settled down for another uncomfortable night on the sloppy fields and slopes of Liberty Gap.

The day had not been entirely quiet at Hoover's Gap but neither had anything of great importance occurred, only the usual bickering which took place any time major elements of the two armies faced each other. Approximately 2:00 a.m., on the twenty-fifth, Kensel's and Andrew's batteries had been moved to the front by Thomas to build up his artillery array. Lilly still had four of his three-inch rifles in position in a depression on the ridge with two more guns in reserve behind a high knob. Major Coolidge had brought his brigade of regulars into the woods on the Union right and Crook had his brigade in reserve. Given the fact that the Union position occupied the narrow end of the funnel of Hoover's Gap there were all the troops on hand which could be deployed. Sometime during the morning Colonel Scribner took the 1st Brigade of Rousseau's Division forward to relieve Major General Joseph J. Reynolds. This move was carried out under a light artillery fire from concealed Confederate batteries and skirmishers fired back and forth at targets of opportunity. Approximately 6:00 p.m., as the day was drawing towards a soggy close, four Southern batteries opened fire, drawing a response from three Union batteries, but nothing was altered by this exchange of fire.[57]

It appears Rosecrans was holding quiet at Hoover's Gap because he was still thinking of Crittenden's as the major blow while Thomas and McCook were noisy feints meant to distract Bragg. If this analysis is correct then Rosecrans was wrong on two points. First, Crittenden was going nowhere, being stuck axle deep in Tennessee mud and, second, Bragg did not know Hoover's Gap and Liberty Gap had been attacked. Astounding as it sounds, Bragg had completely lost command and control of Hardee's Corps, the right wing of his army. This unexplained silence led Bragg to believe the movement of Gordon Granger on Shelbyville was the major Union move, so Bragg focused his attention on Polk's Corps.

There is no adequate explanation for this total breakdown in communication. From army headquarters in Tullahoma, Bragg had direct rail communication with Hardee's headquarters at Wartrace, only 20 miles from Tullahoma. Between Wartrace and Bell Buckle the Confederates had torn up the rail line,[58] shipping the rails south to repair other sections, but Bell Buckle was only five miles from Wartrace and, likewise, the Fairfield Pike connected Wartrace with Hoover's Gap. It seems the Army of Tennessee was using a "don't ask, don't tell" policy. Bragg didn't ask about events and Hardee didn't tell! As to Wheeler, his actions are largely unknown.

Saturday, June 26. Soldiers on both sides must have been wondering if it ever was going to stop raining. Rivers had become torrents while creeks had become rivers and roads had degenerated into bottomless sloughs. At Liberty Gap, General McCook was shifting Sheridan's and Johnson's Divisions toward Hoover's Gap while Brigadier Jeff C. Davis stayed behind with his 1st Division to draw the attention of the defenders away from this move. The 2nd Brigade of that division was commanded by General Carlin who reported he was opposed by three Confederate brigades and three batteries of artillery. These were posted in a strong position about one-half mile from the original Confederate line on June 25.[59] Davis knew he was not to bring on a general engagement, so he kept up only desultory firing. However, Colonel Michael Gooding of the 22nd Indiana commended for bravery First Sergeant William H. Fesler and three other men (unnamed in the report) who "went in advance of the skirmish line to shelter behind a wheat stack. From there he emptied more than one Rebel saddle."[60]

Carlin's estimate of the opposing force was accurate. S. A. M. Wood came up to join Liddell as did Churchill's Brigade. There was skirmish firing all day and twice, Cleburne said, U.S. forces advanced but made no attempt to take and to hold ground. This suited Cleburne just fine because he was short on ammunition. Most of his firing was done by his Whitworth riflemen who struck down mounted men "at distances ranging from 700 to 1,300 yards."[61]

At Hoover's Gap things were beginning to move. Rosecrans decided it did not matter who reached Manchester so long as they did so soon and wore blue uniforms. Approximately 10:00 a.m. Rousseau's 3rd Brigade, the "Regulars," under Major Sidney Coolidge, advanced across a wheat field to pin down the Confederate defenders while the other two of Rousseau's Brigades and all of Major General John Brannon's 3rd Division swung around to outflank the Rebs and cut them off from Fairfield. Brannon's First Brigade, Colonel M. B. Walker commanding, came up against the 17th Tennessee led by Colonel Albert Marks. The 17th had been pushed across Garrison Fork as an advance flank guard by Bushrod Johnson and under this attack the outnumbered Tennesseans began to fall back to the main line.[62]

General A. P. Stewart had no intention of being cut off from Fairfield and he had a pretty good idea what the odds were against him. He was new to command at this level, having been promoted to replace the departed McCown. His division had been pieced together from part of McCown's and part of Breckenridge's and this was their first test of combat as a unit. As the 17th Tennessee was pushed back, Stewart gave the order to fall back toward Fairfield. To cover the retreat Stewart assigned Major Caswell's Georgia Battalion of Sharpshooters and two companies from Colonel R. C. Tyler's 15th/37th Consolidated Tennessee, along with a few cavalry. At first the Union pursuit was rather vigorous so Caswell planned a surprise. A couple of miles from Hoover's Gap the Fairfield Pike came down a bare slope, crossed a creek, and ascended toward a woods line part way up another hill. Sprinting ahead with his infantry Caswell laid an ambush in the trees. When the pursuing Yankees saw the position it looked like a good defensive spot, so they slowed down. When the blue skirmishers reached the woods line with no opposition they all moved out, down the bare slope. Then, Caswell charged the skirmishers and opened a brisk fire on the boys in blue caught in the open. After that, the U.S. advance was rather cautious and took five hours to cover the five miles to Fairfield.[63]

Rain was as much an obstacle as anything provided by the Confederates. Thirty-five years later David M. Moore recalled watching a group of officers ride up to a gun mired in a corn field and wade in to assist, cursing the weather, the mud, the gun team, and especially Rosecrans who, they felt, was responsible for the whole mess. When the gun was moving again the only soldier who had not joined the cursing asked, "Don't you know, you damned fool, that that was Rosecrans pushing the wheel with me?"[64]

Chief of Staff Garfield caught the essence of what had to come next. The left wing of the army needed to make a rapid concentration at Manchester and cut Bragg off from the bridges over Elk River. Only, in the rain, this would not be easy. "A serious mistake has been made by all our commanders in bringing too much baggage," Garfield noted.[65] As Major General Dick Ewell had said the previous year, "The road to glory cannot be followed with much baggage."

Bishop Polk did not attend church on Sunday, June 27. It was to be a day the people of Shelbyville would long remember; indeed, a few speak of it yet. During the night, orders had arrived from Bragg for Polk's Corps to fall back on Tullahoma. Withers' Division left town on the Tullahoma Dirt Road and crossed the Duck River at Skull Camp Bridge, moving towards Thompson's Creek and the present day Raus community. Cheatham led his division across Shofner's Bridge and out the Rowesville Road to a crossroads where the men would turn right for the ascension of the Highland Rim before entering Tullahoma. For part of his muddy 18-mile hike Cheatham would be using the same road needed by Cleburne for his withdrawal from Liberty Gap. Cleburne would use the Rowesville Road for a time but would split off from that road, march through Normandy, and enter Tullahoma via the Gorge Creek Road, now called the Cascade Road. Originally, Bragg had wanted Polk to advance through Guys Gap and attack McCook's flank at Liberty Gap, but the presence of Granger's Union force and the roughness of the country caused Polk to object. When news came of the Union success at Hoover's Gap the plan was moot, and retreat from Shelbyville was the only option.[66]

As the Confederates were leaving the town, Union forces were approaching. Granger had started his Reserve Corps, led by Stanley's cavalry, down the pike from Fosterville towards Guys Gap. About two miles north of the gap Granger ran into some stubborn Confederate skirmishers from Martin's cavalry who checked his advance for some two hours and then suddenly fell back into the earthworks which protected Guys Gap. Private John W. DuBose, one of the Confederate troopers, recorded that they came to the field of battle "in a drenching rain, every man soaked to the skin, nine out of ten rifles too wet to shoot." Colonel James D. Webb's 51st Alabama was at the gap with his advance skirmishers commanded by a Major James T. Dye. As the Confederates fell back to Guys Gap they were joined by Russell's 4th Alabama. The earthworks the Confederate cavalry occupied were formidable, well-designed works and the Yanks were not sure how many Johnnies were inside them. Playing it safe, Stanley placed Colonel Minty with the 4th Regulars in front of the gap and took the 7th Pennsylvania, 4th Michigan, and 3rd Indiana to the right to flank the position. Observing that not much defensive fire was coming out of the place Lieutenant Colonel Galbraith sent forward some men on foot from his 1st Middle Tennessee Cavalry (U.S.), cleared a barricade off the road, and then charged the earthworks mounted. The few Confederates holding the place immediately scattered and for about two miles there was a horse race.[67]

As the Rebel cavalry reached the final ring of defensive works around the town they made a stand. Since the earthworks stretched for miles in both directions across the pike, it was clear they were not all manned. The challenge for the Yanks was to find a place where the works were vacant and to avoid fighting as much as possible. The 3rd Indiana was sent to the left of the road while Major Frank Mix took the 4th Michigan along woods paths to the right until he struck a road where the defenses were vacant. Moving through the works, Mix turned back left towards his original position. The Confederate defenders had a front line in the works facing the 4th Regulars and the 7th Pennsylvania with their left flank refused, or bent back, to confront Mix's command. A sharp fight ensued until the Confederates were attacked in the front by the Regulars and the 7th Pennsylvania. As the Rebs fell back toward Shelbyville a number of them tried to break off from the road and go across country. Unfortunately for them they rode through a gate into a large garden surrounded by a high, stout picket fence and some 250 men were captured.[68]

On the courthouse square Wheeler formed his men for a stand with the courthouse on the left flank and the depot on the right and a battery of four guns was placed to fire down the street along which the Yankees had to advance. Granger paused for a moment to close up the men immediately at hand. Colonel William Sipes with about 150 men of the 7th Pennsylvania were placed in the road in column of fours with the Regulars and the 1st Middle Tennessee in support. Captain Charles Aleshire lined up four pieces of his 18th Ohio Battery, hub to hub, across the pike and, at the word of command, fired a salvo toward the waiting gray troopers. Out of the smoke of the cannon fire, the blue column careened down the road. The Confederate battery fired but most of its rounds went too high and only two Yankee saddles were emptied. The courthouse square echoed with the sound of impact as horses crashed together, men cursed, and guns popped. Most of the guns were Rebel-held; the 7th Pennsylvania had charged with the saber. The encounter must have been brief. Wheeler's right flank near the depot had started breaking for the road to Skull Camp Bridge before the Yankee charge was pressed home.[69] Since Wheeler never filed reports for the Tullahoma campaign, and the Union reports are conflicting, the Confederate loss at Shelbyville is uncertain but Wheeler clearly lost three cannon on the courthouse square and his loss in men captured must have been high.

When the final Confederate stand was made outside the town the 3rd Indiana had been sent to the left to find a way into the village. This unit had followed woods paths left to the Bell Buckle Road and entered Shelbyville by that route. Following alleys and side streets the Indiana troopers passed the right flank of Wheeler's line and were moving along a road to cut off the Southern retreat when they saw Wheeler's men running from the fight on the square. Drawing sabers, the 3rd Indiana charged the gray troopers and a hand-to-hand fight ensued which saw some men from both sides forced into the muddy waters of Duck River.[70]

At some point in the confusion and fighting a staff officer arrived from Bedford Forrest. His command was coming from the

SHELBYVILLE, THE ONLY UNION TOWN OF TENNESSEE.—SKETCHED BY MR. H. R. HÜBNER, THIRD OHIO VOLUNTEERS.—[SEE PAGE 663.]

Shelbyville, Tennessee

Sometimes called "Little Boston." This view is looking north; the Union attack on June 27, 1863, came from beyond the buildings in the background.

area around Columbia and Forrest wanted to know if he could cross the Duck at Skull Camp Bridge. Thinking this represented a definite plan on Forrest's part, Wheeler decided he ought to retake the bridge. To a call for volunteers to re-enter the fight, the 1st Confederate Cavalry responded to a man and this gallant band galloped back across Skull Camp Bridge. By this time the Union troops from the square and those of the 3rd Indiana had joined forces and Wheeler again found himself overwhelmed. With General Martin at his side and many of his men around him Wheeler bypassed the bridge, which had become blocked, and jumped his horse into the river, swimming to safety.[71] Forrest heard the noise of the Yankee attack and crossed the river farther west.

The cavalry fight at Shelbyville shows the growing ascendency of the Union horse in manpower, mounts, and weapons. It is also unusual in featuring two successful saber charges. General Arthur Manigault charges the Confederate cavalry with being very careless about weapons inspections, so that many men went into battle that day with guns rusty and wet from the long continued rain. When charged by the Yankees they could not fire to protect themselves.[72]

Many residents of Shelbyville were very glad to see the Union army arrive, accompanied, as it was, by a locally raised group of galvanized Yankees, the 1st Middle Tennessee. The locale in and around Shelbyville had long been known as "Little Boston" for its antisecession, pro-Union sentiment. One Union trooper recalled "It was at Shelbyville that we were greeted by the pleasant sight of many flags bearing the 'stars and stripes' suddenly flung out of chamber windows and shouts of welcome from women and men who had lived like prisoners in their own homes."[73]

One of those glad to see the Yankees come to town was Miss Pauline Cushman, an actress from Nashville. Miss Cushman had been recruited as a spy by the Union chief of police in Nashville and sent south pretending to be an exile from Federal lines. Posing as a political refugee she gathered and sent back to Nashville what information she could before being discovered and arrested by the Confederates. Condemned to hang, she escaped the noose, she claimed, by pretending to be very sick, too ill to climb the gallows. Actually, when Polk evacuated Shelbyville he sent the amateur spy to the home of a known Union man, Dr. Isaac Blackburn, so she would be safe until the Yankees arrived.[74]

While there must have been many desperate acts of bravery on both sides Union reports mention only three men. Private Mason Brown, 7th Pennsylvania, took a stand on a Shelbyville street corner and fought with a clubbed carbine; Corporal Hofmaster, same regiment, selected an exposed position and fought with his saber; and

Private William Sommers of the 3rd Indiana who captured a Confederate battle flag.[75] There are no Confederate reports on the engagement at Shelbyville.

Granger was satisfied with his day's work and gave his men the task of trying to find some dry place to sleep. Had he been more aggressive an even bigger prize was in his grasp. The wagon trains of both Cheatham and Withers were only a few miles away and were lightly guarded. The same rain which made the progress of the wagons so slow discouraged the Yankee cavalry, and gathering darkness completed the salvation of the trains.[76]

All along their line the Confederates were falling back. About daylight on June 27 at Liberty Gap, Yankee skirmishers moved forward but the move was only designed to cover the withdrawal of the rest of McCook's men. There was no opposition to this gentle push because Cleburne was only interested in holding Bell Buckle long enough to cover his retreat.[77]

Hoover's Gap had been evacuated by Generals Johnson and Bate on Saturday and at 3:30 a.m. Johnson received his orders to fall back to Tullahoma. His command was soon on the road but did not reach Tullahoma, 25-miles away, until 7:00 p.m. This retrograde movement was matched by a slow Union advance. By 10:00 a.m. General Thomas reported having two divisions, Rousseau's and Brannon's, on the road to Fairfield with the road to Manchester open. Thomas was ordered to send the rest of his corps toward Manchester and Sheridan's Division, having come up from Liberty Gap, was sent on the Fairfield Pike. When reaching the old Confederate camps there was a brief skirmish as Sheridan's lead brigade, Laibolt's, bumped into the Rebel rear guard.[78]

Thomas sent the Pioneer Brigade to the front of his column to try to make the road passable but there was still a major ridge of the Highland Rim to climb between Hoover's Gap and Manchester, and a defile called Matt's Hollow had to be traversed, so going was slow. It was dark before the rim was reached and tired, muddy Yankees went into bivouac at the edge of the county seat village. Many of the boys in blue were not impressed by what they saw. One wrote, "This plateau, or shelf of the mountains, is almost as level and flat as a floor, sandy, unproductive soil, producing nothing but Jack oaks . . . the inhabitants are of the lowest order of whites and eke out a miserable existence."[79]

The Confederates were fighting mud and traffic jams as well as skirmishing with Yankees. As Polk's Corps fell back toward Tullahoma some officers interpreted their orders to mean they were to try and save even broken down wagons. This attempt caused Cheatham's Division to move so slowly Cleburne's men began to mingle with the preceding column. Cleburne made some rather sharp remarks about the stupidity of blocking the road, which he was expected to lead a fighting retreat and since the matter made Polk look bad Bragg was all too happy to make his own acidic comments. At any rate, the road cleared.[80]

The town towards which they were headed was well known to many of the bedraggled Rebs since they had been in winter quarters there. Tullahoma had dirt streets and a few dozen small buildings and was less than 15 years old. It had been founded as a construction camp for building the N&C Railroad and still had the rough look of such a place. One of Cleburne's aides had described it as "God-forsaken,"[81] and another Confederate had quipped that the town's name derived from the Latin word *tulla*, meaning mud, and the Greek word *homa,* meaning more mud. On the positive side, there were field fortifications and the depots of supplies amassed there since the last winter. Whether or not Bragg would attempt to hold the place now that the Union forces had reached Manchester was another issue.

As Bragg's army concentrated at Tullahoma that Monday morning Rosecrans was moving his headquarters from Hoover's Gap to Manchester. Before Rosy reached that place a courier handed him a dispatch from Major General George Thomas. Wasting no time, Thomas had sent Wilder's Mounted Infantry towards Decherd and the railroad at first light. Wilder was chosen because his troops had more firepower and greater esprit de corps than the single cavalry brigade available which was commanded by General Ivan Turchin. Actually, Colonel Long commanded the brigade but Turchin headed the division. Turchin's other brigade, Minty's, was at Shelbyville. Besides, Turchin's men were scattered all over Thomas' front as pickets and couriers.[82] By the time Rosecrans arrived at Manchester, Thomas had sent two divisions, Lovell's and Brannon's, down the road halfway to Tullahoma where they went into position along Crumpton's Creek. In the flat, featureless terrain of the Oak Barrens the creek followed a fold in the earth creating a good defensive position on both sides. As the Yanks took position there were only scattered Rebs facing them from the ridge across the creek bottom.[83]

At Manchester, Rosecrans took stock of the condition of his army. His planned main stroke under Crittenden was stuck fast in the mud somewhere near the rural crossroads called Pocahontas. A secondary strike had become his main thrust and, fortunately, this move by Thomas could be supported by McCook, so Rosecrans had a striking force of two army corps with the third coming up, albeit ever so slowly. Only Granger was in a position where he could not be of much use but he certainly was in no danger. But, having achieved a reasonably good position from which he could do Bragg serious damage, time and speed were of the essence. The Army of Tennessee was in the bag but someone had to tie the bag closed, otherwise the Confederates would slip out of the trap. It seemed that the harder Rosecrans tried to move speedily the slower he progressed. Such rains in June were unheard of, the mud was bottomless, and every stream had become a torrent. And still the rain came down.

To Rosecrans it looked as if his own men had conspired to make the problem worse. Despite the orders issued at Murfreesboro about moving light the wagon trains stretched for miles, tying the army down when it needed to fly. From Manchester, Rosecrans addressed the issue. "The General Commanding has noticed with great regret the criminal neglect to obey orders in reference to the reduction of baggage. If this army fails in the great object of the present movement it will be mainly due to the fact that our waggons [sic] have been loaded down with unauthorized baggage. Any Quarter Master caught with unauthorized baggage, such as chairs—usually the fruit of thieving—will be arrested."[84]

Had Rosecrans known how things were going with Wilder he might have felt better, at least at first. Wilder left Manchester going southeast hoping to reach Pelham where he could cross Elk River and proceed to Decherd to attack the N&C Railroad. The river was too high to cross at the usual ford, so the mounted infantry detoured closer to Pelham where there was a bridge. Lieutenant Colonel Kitchell of the 98th Illinois made an attack on the dead run and captured the structure before the Confederates pickets could disable it. A little further on, the South Fork of the Elk had to be crossed, an operation normally accomplished by fording. The state of the river made it necessary to swim the horses across; an old mill nearby was torn down to build a raft to ferry across the mountain howitzers and their ammunition; and the advance continued. At Decherd, Wilder found an alert Confederate garrison of 80 men posted in a stockade and an adjoining railroad cut. After a sharp skirmish Wilder pushed these men back to a wooded ravine and, while they were pinned down, the rest of his command burned the depot, toppled the water tank, and tore up about three hundred yards of track. With Southern reinforcements coming up Wilder found discretion to be a virtue and pulled back into the edge of the mountains.[85] This move broke the railroad for only a matter of a few hours but it sure got Bragg's attention.

For the first time since the campaign had begun Bragg called a council of war to consult with Polk and Hardee. The result of this meeting was a decision to made a stand at Tullahoma, a stand Polk

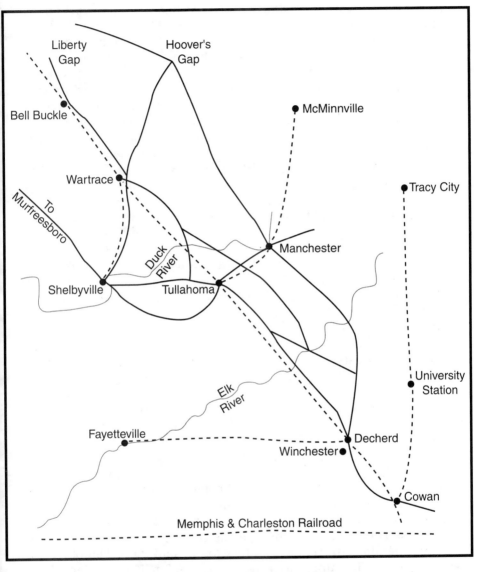

Tullahoma Area, June 29-30, 1863

opposed, fearing the army would be cut off from Chattanooga and forced down into northern Alabama. That area was so barren Polk feared the army would starve before it reached Chattanooga.[86] Polk's objections were overridden and Bragg ordered the "Fighting Bishop" to place five hundred men in Fort Rains to hold that major fortification while Cheatham and Withers set their men to work throwing up breastworks where there were gaps in the line. To aid this move Captain Edward Sayers, chief engineer of Polk's Corps, was ordered to help plan the field works. Sayers replied that Captain Presstman, chief engineer of the Army of Tennessee, had ordered all the available tools sent to General Hardee's sector of the line, so he had nothing to work with. In the end, Cheatham and Withers constructed piles of brush with a little dirt thrown over them.[87] Despite the months during which Tullahoma had been the main supply dump for the army and despite the previous labor there the works around the village were slight and incomplete when the time came to use them.

Once he was forced away from the main line of the railroad at Decherd, Colonel Wilder moved up the main ridge of the Cumberland Plateau to the village of Sewanee, home of the infant University of the South. Following the Brakefield Point Road the column of mounted infantry hit the branch rail line which ran from Cowan, at the foot of the mountain, to Tracy City. This branch line was used primarily to haul coal from mines around Tracy City to Cowan where the coal was used to fuel trains on the main line. After tearing up some track on this branch line Wilder marched a short distance towards Chattanooga but found the main line too heavily guarded to attack. There were persistent rumors that Forrest was after him, so Wilder hid his command in thick woods for the night and, on the June 30, returned via Pelham to Manchester. On his raid no men were lost but only minor damage was done.[88]

In a heavy rain General Thomas was moving major elements of his XIV Corps towards Tullahoma. Crittenden had finally come slogging through the mud, so Thomas had two army corps stacked up behind him and Rosecrans had his army united at last. If Bragg stood at Tullahoma perhaps Thomas could pin him in place while Rosecrans maneuvered other units to outflank him. The objective Thomas had in mind was a temporary defensive position along Crumpton's Creek near Bobo's Crossroads. At Bobo's Crossroads a road from Tullahoma to Hillsboro crossed one leading from Manchester to Winchester. At this point Thomas would be in a good position to destroy the Army of Tennessee if he could mass enough manpower to turn their right flank and cut the railroad. The 4th Division, under Reynolds, camped that night near Concord Church near

Crumpton's Creek while Negley's 2nd Division occupied Bobo's Crossroads. In skirmishing for this position Colonel Thomas Nicholas, 2nd Kentucky Cavalry, U.S., attacked the 4th Tennessee Cavalry commanded by Colonel James Starnes, one of Forrest's more promising officers. After the firing had almost died away a stray bullet struck and killed Starnes.[89] Lt. Col. Charles Lamborn led a scouting party from the 15th Pennsylvania Cavalry, guided by a Negro from a farm house, to within two miles of Tullahoma before encountering opposition. In a charge on a Confederate guard post Lamborn captured 13 men of Colonel W. N. Estes' 3rd Confederate Cavalry and two men of Bragg's escort under Captain Guy Dreux.[90]

Colonel William Innes of the 1st Michigan Engineers was behind the lines but was still performing a duty essential to the success of the campaign and the survival of the army. Confronted with roads which had turned to slush the engineers were repairing the railroad, working outward from Murfreesboro. By June 29 Colonel Innes was headquartered at Bell Buckle where he was confronted by a gap of two and one-half miles between Wartrace and Bell Buckle where the Confederates had removed the rails, no doubt shipping them south to repair other lines. Also to be rebuilt was a 350-foot bridge over the Duck River and a 150-foot trestle at Normandy. The colonel reported to General Rosecrans he would work as fast as he could to open the line. General Granger, now back at the army base of supplies, sent a telegraph message to Rosecrans saying a large train of supplies was leaving Murfreesboro for Manchester. "Heaven knows when it may reach you owing to the bad state of the roads."[91]

Nothing changed on June 30. Rosecrans fought the mud and rain, slowly drawing his army together while his very presence caused Bragg to feel intense pressure. On the other hand, Rosecrans was afraid to move too fast. If Bragg should make an attack with his left, Rosecrans might find his route back to Murfreesboro cut and he would be far from home with nothing to eat. Already the Army of the Cumberland was seeing the bare bottoms of their supply wagons.

General Thomas reported he was occupying a good defensive position along Crumpton's Creek and that he was sending numerous probes out towards Tullahoma. The land was "very flat," Thomas noted, except along the creek. These probes could not have moved very fast, the roads were so bad Lilly's Battery took almost 12 hours to cover 9 miles.[92]

The poor conditions of the roads along with the threat of a more decisive Federal attack on the railroad weighed on Bragg's mind. What should he do? To help make the decision he called another war council at his headquarters, but instead of advice he was asked some probing questions. Polk wanted to know how Bragg proposed to protect the rail line since he obviously did not have enough efficient cavalry to do the job. When Bragg had no other answer than deploying cavalry, Polk informed him that the Union army would have them all cut off in 36 hours. Hardee wanted to strengthen the cavalry line with some infantry but he had never been confident of the army's ability to hold Tullahoma because of the lay of the land. As a result of this meeting Hardee's wagons moved out of town with Polk's following. By 5:00 a.m. on July 1 most of the Army of Tennessee was across Elk River. Ben Seaton of the 10th Texas Cavalry, dismounted, had only been with the Army of Tennessee a few weeks. He was part of Churchill's Brigade which had been captured at Arkansas Post and recently exchanged. Seaton's unit had been assigned to Cleburne's Division and was present at Tullahoma. "We wer ordered to move further on the wright som 2 miles and thar we were in line of battle and thought the fight would come off thar the next day but alas what was the orders—I heard attension batallian in a vary low tone voice—it allmost sounded like a death bell everything was very still and in the distin the bugal softly blows—won culd hardley hear the sound of a voice along the hole line but alas as they were allredy off we started—I new not wher—but soon found out that we wer on a heavy march for the night. We went to Elk River that night some 12 or 15 miles."[93]

Sometime during the morning of Thursday, July 1, Thomas learned from civilians coming into his lines that Bragg was evacuating Tullahoma and so Thomas sent Steedman's 2nd Brigade of Brannon's 3rd Division to occupy the town with Reynolds bringing up the entire 4th Division in support. The rest of the XIV Corps passed to its left flank to try to cut Bragg off before his army could reach the Elk. Around noon four companies of the 39th Indiana Mounted Infantry and four companies of the 2nd Kentucky Cavalry, U.S., commanded by Lt. Col. Elijah Watts came pounding into town, capturing fifteen prisoners. At the same time the 1st Ohio Cavalry formed a column on another road and "charged over an almost impassable abatis of half a mile in width, over a brush breastwork, and into Tullahoma."[94] Up in Pennsylvania, at about the same time, the first shots were being exchanged at Gettysburg, fired, on the Southern side, by men recruited from Tullahoma.

General Brannon followed on into the town and was impressed by what he saw. "The Rebel works were considerable and well constructed, effectively covering the road by which I advanced. They had evidently been abandoned in a great hurry, as I found three large guns and considerable subsistence stores on entering the town. The guns, carriages, and a great portion of the subsistence stores had been set on fire by the rebels and was still burning when I arrived. No ammunition was found. I caused the available subsistence stores to be issued to the troops, being out of rations." Others saw things differently. Henry Campbell of Lilly's Battery said, "The town is a very small and dirty place," while the Cincinnati *Gazette* reporter on the scene styled Tullahoma "a miserable village on a plain as flat as the desert of Sahara." Whatever was left behind was discounted by Bragg. He wired Richmond he had fallen back across Elk River because of threats to his communications but said he had lost nothing of importance.[95]

The railroad and the main road to Decherd, Winchester, and Cowan, and eventually to Chattanooga, crossed Elk River near Estill Springs, also called Allisonia. Benjamin Franklin Cheatham was placed in command at this crossing with orders to destroy the road and rail bridges once all Confederates were across.[96] No action would take place at this crossing, however. Likewise, the nearby Bethpage Bridge was well guarded and only a slight skirmish took place there. The action would come on the flanks despite continuing heavy rains which must have made movement almost impossible.

At 3:00 a.m. on July 3 the division of Phil Sheridan moved through Tullahoma and took the road towards Winchester Springs and a crossing over Elk River. The heavy rains made the river uncrossable on that route without a bridge and the Confederate cavalry made sure there was no bridge. Sheridan turned his column upstream until he reached Rock Creek and, fording this lesser stream, found a useable ford over the Elk. A regiment of Confederate cavalry contested the crossing for a time but superior firepower persuaded them to go away. A cable was then strung across the river and, with its support for the weak and weary, the division crossed the main water barrier separating Rebs and Yanks.[97]

Crittenden finally saw some action on July 2. Pushing Wood's Division out the Hillsboro Road from Manchester, the Yankees learned that the Pelham Bridge used by Wilder some days earlier was still intact. Marching toward the bridge Wood met some Confederate cavalry who did just what they were supposed to do, they fired a few shots to warn the main body and fell back to burn the bridge. The Yankee infantry came right after them, however, and before the fire had taken hold of the bridge timbers many Yanks were rushing over the blazing bridge while others threw the burning flooring off the supports. Wood lost only one man from the 97th Ohio and was able to repair the bridge.[98] Now Bragg had Union troops across the river on both flanks.

The hottest action of the day came at Morris Ferry. Roads from Bobo's Crossroads and Hillsboro both used this crossing of the Elk. Early that morning General Turchin set out to seize this ford. If

successful, the Union advance would have a direct route to Decherd
and Bragg's line of retreat.

Turchin had been down on his luck the entire campaign. Assigned to accompany Crittenden's Corps on what was supposed to
have been the major thrust of the campaign he had lost half his
force on the first day when Rosecrans detached Minty's Brigade and
sent it to the right flank of his army. This left Turchin only Long's
Brigade and most of it had been broken up into pickets and guard
units. On this morning Turchin was leading about five hundred men
accompanied by two James rifles of Stokes Horse Artillery.[99] At Morris Ford the river makes a horseshoe bend with the ford at the head
of the bend. On the east, or Confederate, side of the river were low
hills and a bluff at the water's edge. Inside the bend the land was
flat, although hills marked the edge of the river bottom some 600
yards back from the stream. Waiting for Turchin was the 51st Alabama Cavalry, itching for some revenge for what had happened to
them at Guys Gap and at Shelbyville, the 25th and 26th Tennessee
Infantry, and Darden's Battery.[100]

Turchin sent two companies of the 4th Ohio to test the waters.
A few Rebel pickets fell back in front of them, but as the Yanks got
near the crossing a sharp rifle fire sent them hurrying to cover. The
rest of the regiment dismounted and joined in, but the matter looked
pretty much a stalemate. Turchin had heard of another ford about a
mile and a half upstream, so he sent Lieutenant Shoemaker and his
escort to investigate it. Johnnies were there, too, and Shoemaker
was wounded. Back at Morris Ford, Turchin was ready to attack and
force a crossing when he was hit by enfilade fire from Darden's
previously concealed battery. The whole Yankee force fell back 1,200
yards and settled down to wait. About 2:00 p.m. reinforcements
arrived and their advance found the Southern foot and guns gone.
The 3rd Ohio skirmished with the 51st Alabama, during which affair the Alabama commander, Colonel James D. Webb, lost his life.[101]

After this, the Union force advanced slowly on Decherd, but
they were too late since Bragg's wagons were already beginning to
cross Sewanee Mountain, bound for Chattanooga. This constant
retreat from good positions was wearing Hardee down. Tullahoma
had been vulnerable but he felt the Elk could have been better
defended. At all costs, he wanted to fight at Cowan. That village
was embraced by arms of the mountains and offered many defensive possibilities. At 8:30 p.m. Hardee asked Polk and Buckner to
attend a confidential meeting to discuss the future of the army.
The language of the note dwelt on Bragg's feeble physical condition and the tone is such as to suggest a coup in the making. However, the meeting never came off. One reason was Wheeler who

reported Wilder's Brigade was already atop Sewanee Mountain at University Station and Wheeler feared Union reinforcements were on their way.[102]

As the Confederates fell back on July 3 the Army of the Cumberland flowed forward. Sheridan, led by the 2nd Kentucky Cavalry and the 39th Indiana Mounted Infantry, captured Winchester by mid-morning, fought a small skirmish, and occupied Cowan at the foot of the mountain by 3:00 p.m. Far, far to the northeast the guns fell silent and several thousand Southerners followed Kemper, Garnett, and Armistead across a wheat field toward Cemetery Ridge. Far, far to the southwest the guns roared and several thousand Southerners wondered how much longer they could face another meal of rats or mule meat before they let Grant have Vicksburg.

July 4. Near University Station, on top of Sewanee Mountain, the 5th and 6th Kentucky Cavalry, U.S., skirmished with dismounted men from the 3rd and 4th Georgia. When the Johnnies fell back after an hour's fighting, Lt. Col. Louis Watkins and his Kentucky troopers had captured 15 prisoners and a set of brass musical instruments. The Tullahoma campaign was over.[103] That same day Lee's Army of Northern Virginia retreated from Gettysburg while Grant accepted the surrender of Pemberton's Confederates at Vicksburg.

Chapter Four
The Summary

The first task for the Army of the Cumberland was to occupy the country just gained and to establish control over it. This job was made difficult by the behavior of the Yankee soldiers. At the end of a tense and intensive campaign some letdown in attention to detail and to discipline was expected but the Union troops became rather wild. On July 6 Rosecrans sent out a circular noting that severe depredations on civilians were being committed by U.S. troops. These were to stop and payment was to be made for damages.[1] As good as the commander's word, subordinates began to post guards to protect civilians. The day Rosecrans sent out his initial order Major General Negley ordered Colonel Simel of the 3rd Brigade, 2nd Division, to "furnish such protection to the family of Mr. Bennett (near your camp) as will exclude them from annoyance and trouble from the soldiers of this command." On August 13 Special Order 101 commanded that "the following named officers are appointed to a Board of Appraisers to assess the amount of damage sustained by Mr. John Farris, a citizen of Franklin Co Tenn upon his crops by the Quarter Master and others for the use of this brigade." Detailed to the board were Lieutenants B. Entow, R. E. Wisewall, and John Thoma.[2] Two days later Rosecrans again addressed the commanders of his three corps. Straggling soldiers had been committing outrages on citizens by robbing and thieving, quartermasters were taking forage improperly, and corps commanders were expected to crack down on both practices. The next day, July 9, Sheridan was told to control his troops and to enforce proper discipline. "Disloyalty does not forfeit the rights of humanity which every true soldier will respect."[3] Chief of Staff Garfield summed up the situation quite well in a communication to cavalry commander, General Stanley: "The lawlessness . . . of our soldiers on foraging parties will make bushwhackers faster than any other thing."[4]

Garfield was quite prophetic. On August 3, approximately three miles north of the village of Hillsboro, Private Abner Tull, Company D, 13th Michigan Infantry, was shot by a local civilian, John W. Johnson. A few days later Johnson was arrested and sent to Murfreesboro to be tried by a military commission. He was found guilty of murder and was sent to Nashville where he was hanged at the state penitentiary. A month later, at the same spot, Private William A. Bault, Company A, 3rd Kentucky Infantry, was fired on and killed by another civilian, Alexander P. Anderson. A military commission, presided over by Captain C. A. Thompson of the 19th Michigan Volunteers, found Anderson guilty and sentenced him to five years in the state penitentiary at Nashville.[5] An examination of the *Official Records* and the Union Provost Marshal's Files shows at least a half-dozen guerrilla bands active in the Tullahoma area as late as May 1865 and uncounted citizens who became part-time "Bushwhackers," picking off single Union soldiers or firing into large parties and then running away.

Garrisons were established and expeditions were sent throughout the area. Van Cleve's division was sent to garrison Murfreesboro while Palmer was dispatched to Manchester. Wood occupied Hillsboro with one of his brigades while Beaty went to McMinnville with another, and army headquarters was established at Tullahoma.[6] Colonel Galbraith was sent with his 1st Middle Tennessee Cavalry and the 3rd Ohio to occupy Fayetteville and then to scout on towards Pulaski before turning southeast to Huntsville, Alabama.[7]

Reopening the railroad back to the main supply base at Murfreesboro and Nashville had a high priority. By July 19 McCook had the railroad open to within five miles of Bridgeport on the Tennessee River where the most advanced units of the Army of the Cumberland were stationed. By July 23 the branch line from Cowan to Tracy City was open and coal could reach the main line of the railroad to fuel the engines.[8]

At first, Rosecrans' advance drew little notice. On July 7, after the retreat of Bragg and the Army of Tennessee, Sherman confessed to a newspaperman that he knew nothing of events in Tennessee. Even in Washington the Tullahoma campaign made no impression. On July 5 Stanton telegraphed Rosecrans the news of the Union victories at Gettysburg and Vicksburg. In the course of imparting the news Stanton asked a rhetorical question: "You and your nobel army now have the chance to give the finishing blow to the rebellion. Will you neglect the chance?" Rosecrans promptly replied: "You do not appear to observe the fact that this nobel army has driven the rebels from Middle Tennessee, of which my dispatch informed you. I beg you . . . do not overlook so great an event because it is not written in letters of blood."[9]

"Not written in letters of blood." Is this the reason Tullahoma is the forgotten campaign of 1863? It was the least bloody major campaign of the war. Union casualties for the period June 24 to July 4 were reported as 84 killed, 473 wounded, and 13 captured for a total of 570. Confederate casualties were not completely reported but the number killed and wounded were probably not large; captured was another matter. Major William Wiles, provost marshal for the Army of the Cumberland, reported 1,634 Confederates captured. Of these, 195 were paroled and sent north for the duration of the war while 96 joined the Union army. Some 325 others were sent home, probably because of wounds, and 1,018 were held for exchange.[10]

Rosecrans had been greatly aided by Bragg's poor planning, the collapse of a major part of the Confederate cavalry, and the bickering within the Confederate command structure. The six months the Army of Tennessee stayed in the Tullahoma area was a curious time. Numbers swelled to the largest force the army had ever assembled, then diminished with troops sent to Mississippi and Morgan's Ohio Raid. Organization and drill improved but the inability of the Confederate industrial base to supply the army negated the improvements. Quarrels destroyed all sense of unity and damaged esprit de corps at the command level. Bragg developed no strategy of plan of defense and showed no real interest in holding the last of middle Tennessee still in his hands.

John D. Burtt wrote a brief article for *Strategy and Tactics* magazine in which he touched on the high points of the Tullahoma campaign[11] before raising some questions about the actions of both army commanders. Mr. Burtt commented on the obvious when he says the outcome of the campaign might well have been different if Bragg had not been arguing with his generals, or if the weather had been such that Rosecrans had not gotten stuck fast in the mud.[12] Mr. Burtt misses the mark, however, when he speculates that friendly relations between Forrest and Wheeler would have saved Wheeler from defeat at Shelbyville and might have even resulted in the two smashing the Union cavalry and unleashing Forrest against Rosecrans' supply line.[13]

The fact of the matter is, Wheeler was not even supposed to have been in Shelbyville on June 27; his area of responsibility was on the right flank from Hoover's Gap to McMinnville. Since Wheeler never filed reports for this period no one knows how he came to be on the left flank, but if anyone ordered him there, there is no record of it.

Even if Forrest had cooperated with Wheeler to trap the Union cavalry, Forrest would not have been free to run amuck on the Union supply line. An advance north from Shelbyville would have taken Forrest near the Union forces engaged at Liberty Gap, so close that any mounted infantry there could have given close pursuit. If Forrest had reached Murfreesboro he would have found the town solidly garrisoned by a division of Union infantry, many of them protected by Fortress Rosecrans which also sheltered the Union supply dumps. Neither could the "Wizzard of the Saddle" have wreaked havoc on the wagon trains on the roads. There were none. The mud prevented any wagons being sent forward from Murfreesboro so that Rosecrans' army subsisted on what supplies they had in their trains at the front. Union supplies were running so low that captured Confederate hardtack was issued at Tullahoma. It was not a lack of cooperation between Forrest and Wheeler which lost the Tullahoma campaign for Bragg.

James R. Furqueron, in his article on the Tullahoma campaign, concludes that "the Tullahoma Campaign was Rosecrans' greatest achievement and a classic example of planning and execution . . . that more had not been accomplished was due to a factor over which he had no control: the weather."[14] In a sidebar to this article, Keith Poulter, editor of *North and South* magazine, disagrees. Poulter feels Rosecrans mismanaged his cavalry, which should have been concentrated on his left flank. From that position, Poulter argues, Rosecrans could have launched a lightning strike with his horse soldiers which could have severed Bragg's supply line and cut off his retreat.[15]

Both these positions are short of the truth. Rosecrans had his cavalry just where it had to be if there was to be any chance of Union success. The push towards Shelbyville had to be so heavy that Bragg would conclude that was where the danger lay and focus his attention there. This, and only this, would allow the Union infantry to scale the Highland Rim and turn Bragg's right flank. This is precisely what happened. On June 27, when Polk abandoned Shelbyville and Bragg began a concentration at Tullahoma there was already one Union army corps, Thomas', at Manchester and two others were coming up. Now note, the Yanks at Manchester were closer to Elk River than Bragg was. Had the roads been dry Thomas and Crittenden could have been in position to destroy the Army of Tennessee or to force it south into the Alabama mountains where it would have disintegrated.

Finally, the idea that blue cavalry could have trapped the Army of Tennessee asks too much of the Union cavalry. Rosecrans' mounted arm had improved vastly during the first six months of 1863 but his troopers did not have the firepower or the élan to hold a river line against Reb infantry and artillery. Wilder's Brigade of mounted infantry could have held a bridge, but Stanley's cavalry could not have held the line of the Elk.

The position that the Tullahoma campaign was "a classic of planning and execution" is almost entirely correct. However, it was also a classic of improvisation. Rosecrans intended his far left, under Crittenden, to strike the main blow. When this column literally bogged down, Rosecrans was flexible enough to juggle his plans and improvise a scheme by which Thomas and McCook could trap Bragg. That improvised plan almost worked and, under the circumstances, proved superior to the original plan. It is quite true that Rosecrans could not overcome, or plan for, such weather as he faced. Most likely, June 1863 represents a 500-year record of high rainfall amounts for the Tullahoma area, according to Tennessee Valley Authority (TVA) estimates.

So was the campaign an outstanding success? Yes. The Army of Tennessee escaped and would claim a high price from its opponents at Chickamauga and throughout the Atlanta campaign of 1864. But while strategists of that era always dreamed of destroying the opposing army, that never happened unless the opponent gave up maneuver and occupied a fortified position. The war would not be won by the destruction of armies but by the destruction of the economy which supported the Confederate armies. By occupying middle Tennessee and claiming it for the Union, Rosecrans took an important step toward ending the war.

And the Confederates, what could they claim from the experience of the Tullahoma campaign? At the high command level, very little at all. One may view Polk and Hardee in a somewhat better light than Bragg, but when measured against the larger canvas of Southern independence, all of them had put personal good higher than the good of the cause. None of them had been interested in subordinating personal differences to the overall calling of national independence.

Even at the divisional and brigade level circumstances had allowed for little accomplishment. Cleburne had held his position and had maintained his reputation as a "fighting commander," but we now know he was contending only against a feint. Beyond Cleburne, no divisional or brigade command stands out even as above average. All executed their orders, orders issued by a confused and dispirited command structure, but no single glance of brilliance, no gleam of inspiration marked their performance.

The honors of the Tullahoma campaign, on the Southern side, go to the enlisted men of the Army of Tennessee. They knew their officers were clueless, had been outsmarted; they knew they were facing an ever increasingly better armed and fed enemy whose leaders were maturing in the art of war; yet they remained faithful to the cause to which they had dedicated themselves, the cause of defending family and fireside and faith, and they went on to shed their blood and to expend their valor at Chickamauga, winning for themselves and their army its finest hour. These men, they endured. Better than that cannot be said of many.

General Willich summed up the results of the Tullahoma campaign. "It must be to every thinking mind evident that the tide of the rebellion is turned, its hours are measured."[16] In this assessment Willich was right, though few saw it and agreed at the time. The more obvious Union victories at Gettysburg and Vicksburg absorbed the attention of politicians and the public. Yet one must consider the perspective. Little in the way of food and manpower was reaching the main Confederate armies from the Trans-Mississippi. Grant's capture of Vicksburg, then, did not sever a major supply line which was sustaining the Confederate war effort. Grant did achieve a victory which had important psychological and public relations dimensions, and, since the usual goal of grand strategy at that time was the destruction of the opposing army, Grant fulfilled that goal. But the Confederacy, arguably, could have survived the fall of Vicksburg and still won the war. It did survive for two more years.

General George G. Meade won a defensive victory at Gettysburg. This boosted morale, especially for the Army of the Potomac, which had never known such a clear-cut win, but defensive victories would not win the war. General Robert E. Lee won defensive victories almost every week during 1864 and still wound up at Appomattox.

The Union success in the Tullahoma campaign was obscured by the Confederate triumph at Chickamauga and the later battles at Chattanooga which redeemed the gains that Rosecrans had made in June. But imagine if those gains had never been made. Suppose, despite Vicksburg and Gettysburg, the Campaign of 1864 had begun in the vicinity of Murfreesboro. Would Sherman have been in command or would Grant have been kept in the west? Would Atlanta have been taken before the November elections? Would Lincoln have received a second term? "Might have been" is a game often played by those who love history, but these questions show why the Tullahoma campaign ought not be forgotten.

Notes

CHAPTER ONE

1. This quote is engraved on the wall of the Lincoln Memorial at the entrance to the display hall beneath the statue.
2. James McPherson, *For Cause and Comrades: Why Men Fought in the Civil War*, pp. 122-23; Mark E. Neely, Jr., *The Fate of Liberty*, pp. 60-61; Michael L. Leonard, "Civil War Letters, Ohio Soldiers of Hancock County, 21st Ohio Vols. and 49th Ohio Vols.," p. 18.
3. *Official Records of the War of the Rebellion* (OR), ser. 1, vol. 23, pt. 2, pp. 18, 287, 290-91, 527
4. James A. Connolly, *Three Years in the Army of the Cumberland*, p. 58.
5. Union Provost Marshal (UPM), File of Two or More Citizens, MC416, Roll 41.
6. Ibid., Roll 32.
7. Ibid., Roll 26.
8. William M. Lamers, *The Edge of Glory, A Biography of General William S. Rosecrans*, pp. 258-60, 267.
9. UPM, File of Two or More Citizens, MC345, Roll 27.
10. Ibid., MC416, Roll 80.
11. Ibid., Roll 59.
12. OR, ser. 1, vol. 23, pt. 2, p. 75.
13. Ibid., pp. 270-71.
14. Ibid., pp. 281, 288-89, 300-304.
15. Ibid., pp. 320-21.
16. Ibid., pp. 284-85.
17. Thomas L. Connelly, *Autumn of Glory: The Army of Tennessee, 1862-65*, pp. 70-71.
18. OR, ser. 1, vol. 23, pt. 2, pp. 632-33; Connelly, *Autumn of Glory*, pp. 74-76; Craig L. Symonds, *Stonewall of the West: Pat Cleburne and the Civil War*, p. 116.
19. Ibid., p. 640; Joseph H. Parks, *General Leonidas Polk, CSA, The Fighting Bishop*, p. 300; Connelly, *Autumn of Glory*, p. 72.
20. Connelly, *Autumn of Glory*, p. 84.
21. OR, ser. 1, vol. 23, pt. 2, pp. 652-53; Parks, *Leonidas Polk*, p. 302; Connelly, *Autumn of Glory*, pp. 86-87, 90.

22. Ibid., p. 673; Connelly, *Autumn of Glory*, p. 81.
23. Ibid., p. 722; Symonds, *Stonewall of the West*, p. 122.
24. Ibid., pp. 729-30.
25. Nathaniel Chearis Hughes, *General William J. Hardee: Old Reliable*, p. 47.
26. Stephen Z. Starr, *The Union Cavalry in the Civil War*, vol. 3, "The War in the West," p. 206; Lamers, *Edge of Glory*, p. 248.
27. OR, ser. 1, vol. 23, pt. 2, pp. 3, 10, 12.
28. Ibid., pp. 21-22.
29. Ibid., p. 68.
30. Ibid., p. 111; Jack Hurst, *Bedford Forrest, A Biography*, p. 114.
31. Ibid., pp. 130, 155.
32. Ibid., pp. 203, 241, 296.
33. Ibid., pp. 354-55, 383.
34. OR, ser. 1 vol. 23, pt. 2, pp. 618, 625-26.
35. Ibid., p. 73, pp. 625-26.
36. Ibid., p. 648.
37. Ibid., pp. 661, 665.
38. Ibid., pp. 674-75.
39. Ibid., pp. 688-89.
40. Ibid., p. 700.
41. Ibid., pp. 718-19.
42. Ibid., p. 732.
43. Ibid., p. 741.
44. Ibid., pp. 764, 769.
45. Ibid., p. 770.
46. Ibid., p. 884; Nathaniel C. Hughes, editor, *Liddell's Record, St. John Richardson Liddell, Brigadier General, CSA*, p. 123.
47. Ibid., pp. 54-56, 76, 107-8, 121; Starr, *Union Cavalry*, vol. 3, p. 233; Connolly, *Three Years in the Army of the Cumberland*, p. 100.
48. Ibid., p. 18.
49. UPM, File of Two or More Citizens, MC416, Roll 19.
50. OR, ser. 1, vol. 23, pt. 2, pp. 28-29, 78, 93; Connolly, *Three Years in the Army of the Cumberland*, p. 47.
51. Ibid., p. 132; Connolly, *Three Years in the Army of the Cumberland*, p. 41; Lamers, *Edge of Glory*, p. 252.
52. Ibid., p. 64.
53. Ibid., p. 298.
54. OR, ser. 1, vol. 20, pt. 2, p. 342.
55. Ibid., pp. 379, 574.
56. Ibid., pp. 479, 502-3, 590; UPM, File of Individual Citizens, MC345, Roll 135.
57. Ibid., pp. 614-15, 629.
58. Ibid., pp. 628, 642; Confederate Provost Marshal's Records, General Order #93.
59. Ibid., p. 636.
60. Ibid., p. 642.
61. Ibid., p. 767.
62. Ibid., p. 829.
63. Ibid., p. 873; Connelly, *Autumn of Glory*, p. 110.

64. Ibid., pp. 22-23, 34.
65. Ibid., pp. 45, 95.
66. Ibid., pp. 141, 174, 192; John Rowell, *Yankee Artilleryman*, p. 15. The Spencer was a .52-caliber rifle using a copper rim-fire cartridge. A tube magazine in the stock held seven rounds and extra tubes could be loaded and carried into battle in a specially designed pouch. The cartridges were fed into the chamber by swinging down the trigger guard. The weapon had a range of 2,000 yards.
67. Glen W. Sunderland, *Lightning at Hoover's Gap*, pp. 19, 30.
68. OR, ser. 1, vol. 23, pt. 2, pp. 758-66. Johnston did acknowledge the hand-to-mouth food supply.
69. Ibid., p. 613.
70. Ibid., p. 113.
71. Ibid., p. 650.
72. Ibid., pp. 724, 774.
73. Ibid., p. 762.
74. Ibid., p. 821; Connelly, *Autumn of Glory*, p. 115.
75. Ibid., pp. 632, 642.
76. Ibid., p. 702.
77. Ibid., pp. 663, 691, 730.
78. Ibid., pp. 762 ff.
79. Ibid., pp. 617, 637, 724, 760, 779; H. D. Clayton to his Wife, 23 May 1863, University of Alabama, W. S. Hoole Special Collections, Folder 65, Box 312.

CHAPTER TWO

1. OR, ser. 1, vol. 23, pt. 2, p. 614.
2. Thomas Jordan and J. P. Pryor, *The Campaigns of General Nathan Bedford Forrest*, p. 224.
3. Jordan & Pryor, *Forrest*, pp. 22-26; Hurst, *Bedford Forrest*, p. 113; Robert Selph Henry, *First with the Most*, pp. 124-25; John W. Morton, *The Artillery of Nathan Bedford Forrest's Cavalry*, pp. 75-76.
4. OR, ser. 1, vol. 23, pt. 2, p. 26.
5. Ibid., pp. 623, 625.
6. Jordan & Pryor, *Forrest*, p. 231; OR, ser. 1, vol. 23, pt. 2, p. 701.
7. OR, ser. 1, vol. 23, pt. 2, pp. 624-25, 635.
8. Dee Alexander Brown, *The Bold Cavaliers*, pp. 170-71.
9. Ibid., pp. 168-69.
10. OR, ser. 1, vol. 23, pt. 2, pp. 111-12, 665; Jordan & Pryor, *Forrest*, pp. 233 ff.; Henry, *First with the Most*, pp. 129-31; Morton, *Artillery*, pp. 83-87.
11. Ibid., pp. 664 ff.; Thomas B. Van Horn, *The Army of the Cumberland*, pp. 215-16.
12. Ibid., p. 677.
13. Connolly, *Three Years in the Army of the Cumberland*, pp. 44 f.; James A. Ramage, *Rebel Raider*, p. 152; Van Horn, *Army of the Cumberland*, p. 216.
14. Connelly, *Autumn of Glory*, p. 124.
15. Jordan & Pryor, *Forrest*, pp. 241-43; Hurst, *Bedford Forrest*, p. 115; Henry, *First with the Most*, pp. 133-36; OR, ser. 1, vol. 23, pt. 2, pp. 710, 715.
16. Ramage, *Rebel Raider*, p. 154; OR, ser. 1, vol. 23, pt. 2, pp. 701-2.
17. Streight moved by river from Nashville, Tennessee, to Eastport, Mississippi, and mounted his men on mules. Leaving the river on April 30 he was chased by Forrest night and day across north Alabama. Streight surrendered near

Gaylesville, Alabama, 20 miles short of the railroad bridges at Rome, Georgia, which had been his goal.

18. OR, ser.1, vol. 23, pt. 2, p. 784; Ramage, *Rebel Raider*, pp. 155-56; Connolly, *Three Years in the Army of the Cumberland*, p. 50.

19. OR, ser. 1, vol. 23, pt. 2, pp. 794-95.

20. Ibid., pp. 782-83.

21. Connelly, *Autumn of Glory*, p. 125; R. Lockwood Tower, *A Carolinian Goes to War: The Civil War Narrative of Authur Middleton Manigault*, pp. 76-77.

22. OR, ser. 1, vol. 23, pt. 2, pp. 306-7.

23. Ibid., p. 551.

24. OR, ser. 1, vol. 23 pt. 1, pp. 334 ff.; OR, ser. 1, vol. 23, pt. 2, p. 847.

25. Connolly, *Three Years in the Army of the Cumberland*, pp. 69-70. Connolly includes an interesting story about a deserter from Forrest's command.

26. OR, ser. 1, vol. 23, pt. 1, pp. 352, 356, 358-359, 373-374, 379-380; OR, ser. 1, vol. 23, pt. 2, p. 397 ff., has the account of the spies; Stanley F. Horn, *Tennessee's War*, pp. 191-92.

27. OR, ser. 1, vol. 23, pt. 2, pp. 201, 371; UPM, File of Individual Citizens, MC345, Roll 134.

28. Ibid., pp. 453-54.

29. Ibid., pp. 535, 550.

30. Parks, *Polk*, pp. 293, 313.

31. Hallock, *Bragg*, p. 25.

32. OR, ser. 1, vol. 23, pt. 2, p. 741.

33. Ibid., p. 797.

34. Ibid., pp. 848-49; Connelly, *Autumn of Glory*, pp. 90, 100.

35. Connelly, *Autumn of Glory*, pp. 116-17; Hallock, *Bragg*, p. 14.

36. OR, ser.1, vol. 23, pt. 2, p. 143.

37. Lamers, *Edge of Glory*, p. 264.

38. Ibid., p. 271.

39. OR, ser. 1, vol. 23, pt. 2, pp. 394-95.

40. Ibid., p. 425.

CHAPTER THREE

1. Lamers, *Edge of Glory*, p. 273.

2. OR, ser. 1, vol. 23, pt. 1, pp. 532, 543, 547.

3. Ibid., p. 543; Marshall Thatcher, "A Hundred Battles in the West," cited in *Tennessee's War*, p. 187.

4. Ibid., pp. 523, 528.

5. Ibid., p. 317.

6. Ibid., p. 525; Lamers, *Edge of Glory*, p. 278.

7. Ibid., p. 532; Starr, *Union Cavalry*, vol. 3, p. 238.

8. Ibid., pp. 533, 544, 547.

9. Ibid., p. 544; Starr, *Union Cavalry*, vol. 3, p. 238. Wheeler never filed reports for the Tullahoma campaign, so the Confederate perspective of these events cannot be recounted.

10. OR, ser. 1, vol. 23, pt. 1, pp. 521, 528; Connelly, *Autumn of Glory*, pp. 118-19.

11. Ibid., p. 524.

12. Ibid., pp. 521, 580; Lamers, *Edge of Glory*, p. 283.

13. Ibid., p. 519.
14. Ibid., p. 594.
15. Ibid., pp. 587-88.
16. Ibid., pp. 588-89, 594-95.
17. Authur J. L. Freemantle, *Three Months in the Southern States*, pp. 155-56 passim.
18. OR, ser. 1, vol. 23, pt. 1, pp. 465, 600.
19. Ibid., p. 594.
20. Ibid., p. 599.
21. Ibid., p. 507.
22. Ibid., pp. 483, 486.
23. Ibid., p. 494.
24. Ibid., pp. 495-96.
25. Ibid., pp. 505-7.
26. Ibid., p. 498.
27. Ibid., pp. 588, 595; Hughes, *Liddell's Record*, p. 127.
28. Ibid., p. 588.
29. Ibid., pp. 457-58.
30. Ibid., p. 458; Connelly, *Autumn of Glory*, p. 118.
31. Ibid., p. 455.
32. John W. Rowell, *Yankee Artilleryman: Through the Civil War with Ely Lilly's Indiana Battery*, p. 25; Sunderland, *Lightning at Hoover's Gap*, p. 31.
33. OR, ser. 1, vol. 23, pt. 1, pp. 455, 458; Rowell, *Yankee Artilleryman*, p. 77; Sunderland, *Lightning at Hoover's Gap*, pp. 18-19.
34. Ibid., p. 611; Stanley Horn, ed., *Tennesseans in the Civil War*, vol. 1, p. 173, passim.
35. Ibid., pp. 611-13.
36. Ibid., p. 458.
37. Ibid., pp. 455, 458; Rowell, *Yankee Artilleryman*, p. 65.
38. Connolly, *Three Years in the Army of the Cumberland*, p. 92.
39. OR, ser. 1, vol. 23, pt. 1, pp. 612-13.
40. Horn, *Tennesseans in the Civil War*, vol. 1, p. 254 passim.
41. OR, ser. 1, vol. 23, pt. 1, pp. 602-3. The "conical hill" spoken of in this report was completely removed during the construction of Interstate 24 which today slices completely down the middle of the site of the Hoover's Gap engagement.
42. OR, ser. 1, vol. 23, pt. 1, pp. 455, 459; Rowell, *Yankee Artilleryman*, pp. 82-83.
43. Walter T. Durham, *Rebellion Revisited*, p. 179.
44. OR, ser. 1, vol. 23, pt. 1, pp. 533, 536.
45. Ibid., p. 567.
46. Ibid., pp. 589, 597.
47. Ibid., pp. 449, 487.
48. Ibid., p. 487.
49. Ibid., pp. 490-91, 595.
50. OR, ser. 1, vol. 23, pt. 1, pp. 487, 490-91, 496-97.
51. Ibid., pp. 484, 502-3.
52. Symonds, *Stonewall of the West*, p. 127.
53. OR, ser. 1, vol. 23, pt. 1, pp. 589, 590.

54. Ibid., pp. 499-500.

55. Ibid., pp. 499-500, 505.

56. Ibid., pp. 479, 502-3, 590; Hughes, *Liddell's Record,* p. 127.

57. Ibid., pp. 434, 455.

58. Ibid., p. 503.

59. Ibid., pp. 463-64, 480.

60. Ibid., pp. 470-71, 478.

61. Ibid., pp. 587, 590.

62. Ibid., pp. 440-41, 604.

63. Ibid., pp. 430, 604, 614.

64. Lamers, *Edge of Glory,* pp. 281-82.

65. OR, ser. 1, vol. 23, pt. 1, p. 470.

66. Ibid., pp. 583, 618-19.

67. Ibid., p. 536; Horn, *Tennessee's War,* pp. 184-85.

68. Ibid., pp. 557, 561.

69. Ibid., pp. 559-60, 565-66; Starr, *Union Cavalry,* vol. 3, p. 245.

70. Ibid., pp. 559-60.

71. Ibid., p. 536; John P. Dyer, *From Shiloh to San Juan: The Life of "Fightin' Joe" Wheeler,* p. 84. It is unclear what blocked the bridge. Various accounts say a cannon, a caisson, or a wagon overturned or broken through the flooring. At any rate, it was blocked. Legend has it that Wheeler jumped his horse off a high bluff into the flooded river. Unfortunately for legend, there are no bluffs anywhere near Skull Camp Bridge. The banks of the river are only two to three feet high at normal river stage and, with the river in flood, there would have been no banks at all. At flood stage the Duck River would have been only 60 or 75 feet wide at most.

72. Tower, *A Carolinian Goes to War,* p. 74.

73. Thatcher, "A Hundred Battles in the West," cited in Horn, *Tennessee's War,* p. 186.

74. Horn, *Tennessee's War,* pp. 186-87.

75. OR, ser. 1, vol. 23, pt. 1, pp. 562, 566.

76. Ibid., p. 620.

77. Ibid., pp. 471, 591.

78. Ibid., pp. 425, 466-67, 608.

79. Ibid., pp. 580-81; Rowell, *Yankee Artilleryman,* p. 84.

80. Ibid., p. 619.

81. Symonds, *Stonewall of the West,* p. 825.

82. OR, ser. 1, vol. 23, pt. 1, p. 426; Starr, *Union Cavalry,* vol. 3, p. 239.

83. Ibid., p. 426.

84. Ibid., pp. 478-79.

85. Ibid., pp. 460-61.

86. Ibid., p. 621.

87. Ibid., pp. 621-22, 891.

88. Ibid., p. 461.

89. Ibid., pp. 425, 569.

90. Ibid., pp. 577-78.

91. Ibid., p. 583.

92. Ibid., pp. 427, 486; Rowell, *Yankee Artilleryman,* p. 86.

93. Ibid., pp. 622-23; Harold B. Simpson, ed., *The Bugle Softly Blows: The Confederate Diary of Benjamin M. Seaton,* p. 35.
94. Ibid., pp. 428, 467, 570, 572.
95. Ibid., pp. 453, 483; Rowell, *Yankee Artilleryman,* pp. 86-87.
96. Ibid., p. 623.
97. Ibid., p. 467.
98. Ibid., pp. 520, 525.
99. Ibid., pp. 554, 568.
100. Ibid., pp. 554, 608-9.
101. OR, ser. 1, vol. 23, pt. 1, pp. 555, 574.
102. Ibid., pp. 615, 623.
103. Ibid., p. 550.

CHAPTER FOUR

1. OR, ser. 1, vol. 23, pt. 2, p. 517.
2. UPM, File of Individual Citizens, MC345, Roll 89.
3. OR, ser. 1, vol. 23, pt. 2, pp. 521, 525.
4. Ibid., pp. 526-27.
5. UPM, File of Individual Citizens, MC345, Roll 79. Private Tull is buried in grave H-3059 at Stones River National Cemetery, Murfreesboro, Tenn.; UPM, File of Individual Citizens, MC345, Roll 5. Private Bault is buried in grave H-3060 at Stones River National Cemetery, Murfreesboro, Tenn.
6. OR, ser. 1, vol. 23, pt. 2, p. 522.
7. Ibid., p. 542.
8. Ibid., pp. 543-44.
9. Ibid., p. 518.
10. Ibid., pp. 424-25.
11. John T. Burtt, "War by Maneuver: The Tullahoma Campaign, June 1863," *Strategy and Tactics,* issue #183, Nov./Dec. 1996, pp. 52-62.
12. Burtt, "War by Maneuver," p. 62.
13. Burtt, "War by Maneuver," p. 62.
14. James R. Furqueron, "A Fight or a Footrace: The Tullahoma Campaign," *North & South: The Magazine of Civil War Conflict,* January 1998, Issue 2, p. 89.
15. Ibid., p. 38.
16. OR, ser. 1, vol. 23, pt. 2, p. 489.

Bibliography

Baumgartner, Richard A. *Blue Lightning: Wilder's Mounted Infantry Brigade in the Battle of Chickamauga.* Huntington, W.Va.: Blue Achorn Press, 1997.

Brown, Dee Alexander. *The Bold Cavaliers. Morgan's 2nd Kentucky Raiders.* Philadelphia: J. B. Lippencott Company, 1959.

Burtt, John T. "War by Maneuver: The Tullahoma Campaign, June 1863." *Strategy and Tactics,* issue 183 (Nov./Dec. 1996), pp. 52-62.

Connelly, Thomas Lawrence. *Autumn of Glory: The Army of Tennessee, 1862-1865.* Baton Rouge: Louisiana State University Press, 1971.

Connolly, James A. *Three Years in the Army of the Cumberland.* Ed. by Paul M. Angel. Bloomington: Indiana University Press, 1959.

Durham, Walter T. *Rebellion Revisited.* Nashville: Sumner County Museum Association, 1982.

Dyer, John P. *From Shiloh to San Juan: The Life of "Fightin' Joe" Wheeler.* Baton Rouge: Louisiana State University Press, 1989.

Feis, William B. "The Deception of Braxton Bragg." *Blue and Gray Magazine* (October 1992), p. 10 ff.

Fremantle, Lt. Col. Arthur J. L. *Three Months in the Southern States.* Lincoln: University of Nebraska Press, 1991. Reprinted from the 1864 edition.

Furqueron, James R. "A Fight or a Footrace: The Tullahoma Campaign." *North & South: The Magazine of Civil War Conflict,* issue 2 (January 1998), pp. 28-38, 82-89.

Hallock, Judith Lee. *Braxton Bragg and Confederate Defeat.* Tuscaloosa: University of Alabama Press, 1991.

Henry, Robert Selph. *First with the Most Forrest.* Jackson, Tennessee: McCowat-Mercer Press, 1944.

Horn, Stanley F. *Tennessee's War, 1861-1865.* Nashville: Tennessee Civil War Commission, 1965.

Horn, Stanley F., ed. *Tennesseeans in the Civil War.* 2 vols. Nashville: Civil War Centennial Commission, 1964.

Hughes, Nathaniel Chearis. *General William J. Hardee: Old Reliable.* Wilmington, N.C.: Broadfoot Publishing Company, 1987.

———. *Liddell's Record. St. John Richardson Liddell, Brigadier General, CSA.* Dayton, Ohio: Morningside Press, 1985.

Hurst, Jack. *Nathan Bedford Forrest: A Bibliography.* New York: Alfred A. Knopf, 1993.

Jordan, Thomas, and J. P. Pryor. *The Campaigns of General N. B. Forrest.* New York: De Capo Press, 1996. Originally printed 1867.

Lamers, William M. *The Edge of Glory: A Biography of General William S. Rosecrans, USA.* New York: Harcourt, Brace, & World, Inc., 1961.

Leonard, Michael L. "Civil War Letters, Ohio Soldiers of Hancock County, 21st Ohio Vols. and 49th Ohio Vols." Aurora, Colorado: Privately printed, 1995. Collection of the author.

McPherson, James. *For Cause and Comrades: Why Men Fought in the Civil War.* New York: Oxford University Press, 1997.

Morris, Ray. "The Steadiest Body of Men I Ever Saw." *Blue and Gray Magazine,* (October 1992), p. 32 ff.

Morrow, John Anderson. *The Confederate Whitworth Sharpshooters.* Privately Published. N.p., 1989.

Morton, John Watson. *The Artillery of Nathan Bedford Forrest.* Marietta, Ga.: R. Bemis Publishing Co., 1995. Originally published 1909.

Neely, Mark E., Jr. *The Fate of Liberty: Abraham Lincoln and Civil Liberties.* New York: Oxford University Press, 1991.

Official Records of the War of the Rebellion. Washington: U.S. War Department, 1880-1901.

Parks, Joseph H. *General Leonidas Polk, CSA, The Fighting Bishop.* Baton Rouge: Louisiana State University Press, 1962.

Ramage, James A. *Rebel Raider: The Life of General John Hunt Morgan.* Lexington: University of Kentucky Press, 1986.

Rowell, John W. *Yankee Artilleryman: Through the Civil War with Ely Lilly's Indiana Battery.* Knoxville: University of Tennessee Press, 1975.

Simpson, Harold B. *The Bugle Softly Blows: The Confederate Diary of Benjamin M. Seaton.* Waco, Texas: Texian Press, 1965.

Starr, Stephen Z. *The Union Cavalry in the Civil War.* 3 vols. Baton Rouge: Louisiana State University Press, 1985.

Sunderland, Glen W. *Lightning at Hoover's Gap.* New York: Thomas Yoseloff, 1969.

Symonds, Craig L. *Stonewall of the West: Patrick Cleburne and the Civil War.* Lawrence: University Press of Kansas, 1997.

Tower, R. Lockwood. *A Carolinian Goes to War: The Civil War Narrative of Arthur Middleton Manigault.* Columbia: University of South Carolina Press, 1983.

Union Provost Marshal Files. Microfilm. Tennessee State Library and Archives.

Van Horn, Thomas B. *The Army of the Cumberland.* Originally published 1875. New York: Smithmark, 1996.

Williams, Samuel Cole. *General John T. Wilder, Commander of the Lightning Brigade.* Bloomington: Indiana University Press, 1936.

Index

First names are given where known.